The Russian Church and the Papacy

VLADIMIR SOLOVIEV

The Russian Church
and the Papacy

An Abridgment of
Russia and the Universal Church

Foreword by Christoph Cardinal Schönborn, O.P.
Preface by Scott Hahn
Edited by Fr. Ray Ryland
Translated by Herbert Rees

CATHOLIC ANSWERS
SAN DIEGO
2001

Published by Catholic Answers, Inc.
2020 Gillespie Way
El Cajon, CA 92020
(888) 291-8000 (orders)
(619) 387-0042 (fax)
www.catholic.com (web)
Cover design by Mary Lou Morreal
Printed in the United States of America
ISBN 1-888992-29-8

Contents

Foreword

Between the thought and concerns of Pope John Paul II and the eminent Russian philosopher and theologian, Vladimir Soloviev, there are a number of significant parallels. When the Holy Father commends the writings of Soloviev and speaks of him as a prophetic figure, he is pointing us to a man who is a kindred spirit of his.

In 1995 John Paul II issued his landmark apostolic letter, *Orientale Lumen*, to help Catholics better understand the vast rich heritage of the separated Eastern Churches. Never before in Christian history has a leader of one tradition written so appreciatively, so incisively, about the heritage of another tradition as has the Holy Father.

Never before, that is, with the exception of Vladimir Soloviev's *Russia and the Universal Church*, of which the present volume is an abridgment. Though John Paul's description of the Eastern ethos is more detailed, it is not more warmly and accurately done than is Soloviev's description of the Catholic Church and especially of the office of Peter.

For centuries, Roman pontiffs have reached out to the separated Eastern Churches, urging them in most irenic terms to return to communion with Rome. No pontiff has so extended himself, none has written and spoken so eloquently, as John Paul II. Unfortunately, to this consistent papal outreach there has never been a corresponding positive response from the hierarchies of the Eastern Orthodox Churches.

Never, that is, until Vladimir Soloviev (acting on his own authority, of course) exhorted the separated Eastern Churches warmly to grasp the outstretched hand of Rome in restored communion. The basic theme of his book is that the Eastern Churches can never become truly themselves, truly Catholic, until they are reconciled with Rome.

7

Magisterial statements aimed at the separated Eastern Churches have always insisted that the Eastern traditions must be preserved. "Unity in legitimate diversity"[1] has been the hallmark of the Church's appeal for reconciliation with the Orthodox Churches. Yet prelates and theologians of those Churches seem never to have taken the Catholic Church's reassurance at face value.

Never, that is, until Vladimir Soloviev responded wholeheartedly. In Rome's outreach, said Soloviev, "we are not asked to change our nature as Easterns or to repudiate the specific character of our religious genius." Again, "We merely have to restore to our religion its catholic or universal character by recognizing our oneness with the active part of the Christian world [by which term he designates the Catholic Church], with the West centralized and organized for a universal activity and possessing all that we lack." To accomplish this, "there is no need to invent or create anything new."

In accord with the agenda for the Jubilee Year,[2] on March 12, 2000, John Paul II spoke on behalf of the Catholic Church, asking pardon of God and of all other persons who have suffered at the hands of the sons and daughters of the Church. Never before had a pontiff, or any other prominent religious leader, issued such a far-reaching statement of repentance on behalf of his own tradition.

Never before, that is, with the exception of Vladimir Soloviev's *mea culpa* spoken (again, on his own authority) on behalf of the Russian and other Orthodox Churches. A recent commentator speaks of Soloviev as "a prophet of ecclesial repentance."[3] Readers of this book will be impressed and enlightened by the solemn manner in which Soloviev calls the roll of sins and shortcomings of the separated Eastern traditions.

In 1992 the Congregation for the Doctrine of the Faith, with

---

[1] *Ut Unum Sint*, 54.

[2] Set forth in John Paul II, *Incarnationis Mysterium* (1998).

[3] Robert F. Slesinski, "V. S. Solovyov: The Centenary of a Death," *Communio* 26, Winter 1999, 786.

approval of John Paul II, issued *Communionis Notio* (Letter to the Bishops of the Catholic Church on Some Aspects of the Church Understood as Communion). Section 17 emphasized the Church's teaching that communion with Peter's successor is "not an external complement to the particular church, but one of its internal constituents. . . ." Therefore, the existence of the separated Eastern Churches ("those venerable Christian communities") is "wounded" by their separation. Soloviev's book confirms this diagnosis. Every major fault he discerns in the life of the Orthodox Churches he traces back to their separation from Rome.

In recent years it has become customary to speak of the Catholic Church and the Eastern Orthodox Churches as "sister Churches." John Paul II approved a clarification of this term in a *Note on the Expression "Sister Churches"* issued by the Congregation for the Doctrine of the Faith (2000). According to section 11, the term may be used properly only when referring to particular Churches. "It must always be clear . . . that the one, holy, Catholic, and apostolic universal Church is not sister but mother of all the particular Churches."

Soloviev would have understood and agreed with this distinction. In line with the precision stated in this Note, he never refers to "our two Churches." The phrase "the universal Church," which he used often, always refers to the Roman Catholic Church. Practically alone among Eastern Orthodox writers, Soloviev saw the true relation of the separated Eastern Churches to the Catholic Church. *Orientale Lumen* teaches that the tradition of the Eastern Churches "is an integral part of the heritage of Christ's Church . . ." (1). Soloviev said essentially the same. We Orthodox Christians, he wrote, must "recognize ourselves for what we are in reality, an organic part of the great body of Christendom. . . ." There is in Soloviev no hint of the claim made by Eastern Orthodox apologists, that the Orthodox Churches as a whole constitute the one true Church.

Consider one final indication of the spiritual kinship between John Paul II and Vladimir Soloviev. When Christ founded his Church on Peter the rock, says Soloviev, he established "the

unique institution of universal fatherhood in the Church. . . ."
He thereby entrusted "the universal Church" to Peter "as the
one supreme representative of the divine fatherhood to the whole
family of the sons of man."Therefore, he insists, "Love for the
Church has no real meaning except for those who recognize perpetually in the Church a living representative and a common father of all the faithful, capable of being loved as a father is loved
in his family. . . ."

This universal fatherhood about which Soloviev writes so eloquently: has any other pontiff so fully exemplified this fatherhood
as has John Paul II?

—Christoph Cardinal Schönborn, O.P.
Archbishop of Vienna

Preface

From the East he came, appearing suddenly, nearly a century after his death, in Church documents of the highest authority. For many Westerners, Vladimir Soloviev made his debut in *Fides et Ratio* (Faith and Reason), the 1998 encyclical letter of Pope John Paul II. There his name emerges in a sweeping genealogy of the great Christian philosophers, from St. Augustine and St. Thomas Aquinas to Newman and St. Edith Stein. Two years later, the same Pope would praise Soloviev as one of the modern era's great "witnesses of the faith and illustrious Christian thinkers" and call his work "prophetic."

Who was that man, and how did he elude popular notice for so long?

Vladimir Sergeyevich Soloviev (1853–1900) was hardly unknown in his own time and place. Recognized during his lifetime as the leading light in a brilliant constellation of Russian thinkers, he developed his thought not only in scholarly publications, but in popular journalism and even in fiction. He was a close friend of the novelist Fyodor Dostoyevsky and perhaps his greatest influence.

As a philosopher, Soloviev was fearless. He ranged in dark valleys where other Christians feared to venture. He actively engaged the works of Rousseau, Kant, Hegel, Nietzsche—not to mention the ancient Gnostics and the various schools of Buddhism. He did this not to concoct a semi-Christian syncretism, but to demonstrate that the Holy Spirit is active throughout the history of human thought, guiding its development, in spite of humanity's sin and moral and intellectual blindness.

Soloviev's early work was marked by an almost effervescent optimism, which flowed from a mystical experience he had had in his youth. It was a vision of "Sophia"—the wisdom of God, the eternal object of God's love, and love perfected in life-giving splendor. Thus enlightened, he was able to see the kernels of truth in all systems of thought and to extract those good things in order to restore them from God. He accomplished this restoration in his own systematic work, which was an architectonic marvel. Hans Urs von Balthasar praised Soloviev for his "skill in the technique of integrating all partial truths in one vision" and ranked him second only to Thomas Aquinas as "the greatest artist of order and organization in the history of thought."[1]

The great obstacle to divine-human progress, he believed, was the fragmentation of the Church. Though he was baptized, raised, and reached his maturity in the Russian Orthodox church, Soloviev eventually concluded that truth reached its fullness neither in the ossified tradition of Byzantine Orthodoxy nor in the unbridled prophetic character of Protestantism, but in the unity that is accomplished only under the authority of St. Peter: the papacy.

In a stunning confession of faith, he wrote:

> As a member of the true and venerable Eastern or Greco-Russian Orthodox church, which speaks neither through an anti-canonical synod nor through the employees of the secular power, but through the utterance of her great Fathers and Doctors, I recognize as supreme judge in matters of religion him who has been recognized as such by St. Irenaeus, St. Dionysius the Great, St. Athanasius the Great, St. John Chrysostom, St. Cyril, St. Flavian, the Blessed Theodoret, St. Maximus the Confessor, St. Theodore of the Studium, St. Ignatius, and on and on—namely, the apostle Peter, who lives in his successors and who has not heard our Lord's words in vain: "You are Peter, and on this rock I will build my church" (Matt. 16:18); "Strengthen your brethren" (Luke 22:32); "Feed my sheep, feed my lambs" (cf. John 21:15, 16, 17).

Soloviev's vision was expansive, ecumenical, universalist— "catholic" is the most appropriate term. If it was overwhelm-

---

[1] Hans Urs von Balthasar, *The Glory of the Lord: A Theological Aesthetics*, vol. 3: *Studies in Theological Styles: Lay Styles* (San Francisco: Ignatius Press, 1986), 284. This long essay is perhaps the best readily available evaluation of Soloviev's writings as a whole—ED.

ingly optimistic in his early work, it was not naïve. He invoked history to show how world powers had formerly acted, through the guidance of the Holy Spirit, to advance the gospel. Again, the Spirit accomplished this work in spite of the sin and blindness of emperors from Constantine to Charlemagne. Nor was Soloviev uncritical in his devotion to the papacy. He held the office, and particular popes, to high standards, and was unsparing in his judgment of their failures to act as humble servants.

He held a great hope that Russia—reunited to the Catholic Church—would emerge as the next temporal instrument of divine Providence and establish a "free and universal theocracy," where humanity could live in the freedom of the children of God. Within this vision, he advanced some radical notions for his time. He promoted religious liberty, for example, and he opposed the death penalty.

In later works, Soloviev tempered his early optimism with the biblical realism of Revelation. The coming century, he believed, was to witness the advance of the Antichrist. It would be wrong, however, to conclude that Soloviev had turned pessimist. For he believed that the encroaching darkness would, in spite of itself, serve God's purposes. In a dark time, the dispersed elements of light would appear in stunning chiaroscuro. The advance of the Antichrist would be the precondition of the reunion of Christianity's dispersed members—Protestant and Orthodox—under papal authority.

Soloviev, like Thomas Aquinas, died young, not yet fifty years of age. His last days are shrouded in controversy. Ten years after his death, a Russian priest wrote that he had heard the philosopher's last confession and given him Communion. As a Catholic, Soloviev certainly had the right to resort to an Orthodox priest for the last rites if no Catholic priest were available. Yet the priest also claimed to recount some of the details of the dying man's confession, including the recantation of Soloviev's allegiance to the pope. Friends of Soloviev expressed doubts, and others were rightly hesitant to accept as trustworthy the witness of a priest who would violate the seal of the confessional. For Soloviev, Catholicism represented more than just a decision at the end of his life; it was the thrust of his work for two decades of his life. In any event, whether or not he voluntarily returned to the Orthodox church is irrelevant to a consideration of his views.

This was the judgment of Pope John Paul II, and it is the judgment of an increasing number of eminent Catholics who recognize Soloviev (in the words of one biographer) as the Russian Newman.

In the reemergence of this great Russian voice, I believe we can see the working of the Holy Spirit, the blessed "progress" Soloviev himself foresaw.

—Scott Hahn

Introduction

Once upon a time there lived a giant in Russia. Unlike the giants we read about in fairy tales, this giant was fully human; he lived from 1853 to 1900. He was an unusual giant, a genius with an astonishing range of intellectual and spiritual gifts. Biographers credit him with being philosopher, political thinker, theologian, literary critic, poet, prophet, mystic. Yet this giant is largely unknown in the West today. His name is Vladimir Soloviev (variously transliterated "Solovyov" or "Solovyev").

This giant came from a cultured and religious family. His grandfather was a Russian Orthodox priest, his father was an eminent historian and professor at Moscow University. Soloviev was an intimate friend of Fyodor Dostoyevsky. Indeed, Soloviev was the model for one of Dostoyevsky's most memorable and admirable characters, Alyosha Karamazov, in *The Brothers Karamazov*.

Soloviev's career as university professor was cut short abruptly when he dared publicly to plead with the tsar to forgive an assassin who had attempted to kill the tsar. During and after his academic career, Soloviev published many works of philosophy, logic, metaphysics, theology, and theosophy (the integration of theology and philosophy). Through it all, Soloviev lived a life of Franciscan simplicity. He was almost always penniless from emptying his wallet to anyone who asked him for help. If an indigent approached him when Soloviev had no money, he would give the needy person his own coat. On occasions he even gave beggars his shoes. As a result, he continually had to borrow clothes from his friends. His premature death apparently was caused by overwork and by the physical consequences of his radical self-denial.

The purpose of this abridgment is to make available one aspect of Soloviev's thought, namely, his insights into the nature of Christian unity and the basic issue of authority which underlies all disunity among Christians. As a member of the Russian

Orthodox church, he made valiant efforts to reconcile the Eastern Orthodox churches to Rome. Speaking of Soloviev's ecumenical endeavors, von Balthasar praises the "clarity, verve, and subtlety" of his "brilliant apologia" for the papacy. Von Balthasar further declares that "it belongs amongst the masterpieces of ecclesiology."[1] In *Fides et Ratio* (74), Pope John Paul II singled out Soloviev as a source of enrichment for Catholic thought.

A Russian Orthodox theologian, Georges Florovsky, has praised Soloviev for his passion for Christian unity. Soloviev, says Florovsky, regarded the reunion of Christendom, and especially the reconciliation between the Eastern Orthodox churches and Rome, as "the central problem of Christian life and history." Florovsky calls Soloviev's contribution to the discussion on Christian unity "momentous."[2]

Only during the last two decades of his brilliant career did Soloviev focus his attention on Christian unity. In 1886 he submitted to Croatian Bishop Strossmayer a proposal for reuniting the Russian Orthodox church with the Roman Catholic Church. The archbishop was deeply impressed. He commended Soloviev to the papal nuncio in Vienna and arranged for an audience with Pope Leo XIII. At that audience in the spring of 1888, the Pope gave Soloviev the papal benediction in recognition of his efforts at reconciling the Russian church to the Catholic Church.[3]

Soloviev made several trips to Europe to confer with representatives of Eastern Catholic churches and with Jesuit theologians. By 1886 his reunion activities were widely recognized and,

---

[1] Hans Urs von Balthasar, *The Glory of the Lord: A Theological Aesthetics*, vol. 3: *Studies in Theological Styles: Lay Styles* (San Francisco: Ignatius Press, 1986), 334.

[2] Georges Florovsky, "The Orthodox Churches and the Ecumenical Movement Prior to 1910," *A History of the Ecumenical Movement, 1617–1948* (Ruth Rouse and Stephen Neill, eds., Philadelphia, 1967), 214.

[3] Peter P. Zouboff, *Vladimir Solovyev's Lectures on Godmanhood* (International University Press, 1944), 31.

in Russian official circles, strongly condemned. Both the Russian church and the Russian imperial government banned him from all public activities. They said his work was harmful to the Russian imperial regime and to the [Orthodox] church of Russia.

At this point, Soloviev seriously considered entering a Russian monastery. He decided against it because the monastic authorities would not allow him to continue his pro-Catholic activities. At the request of a French Jesuit, Soloviev wrote in French a summary of his ideas about the Church and the key issue of doctrinal authority. That book is *Russia and the Universal Church*, of which this present work is an abridgment.

Only those portions of Soloviev's book which deal with ecclesiological issues are included in this abridgment. The text here set forth is entirely the words of Soloviev in translation from the French. The divisions of the material selected and the headings given to each of the four parts have been added for clarification. Chapter titles in part one have been added. The chapter headings in part two are taken from Soloviev's book. These chapters deal with issues in the Russian Orthodox church in the nineteenth century. They are necessary background for following Soloviev's line of thought about the papacy. In part three, except for the term "preamble," all of Soloviev's chapter headings have been retained. Finally, part four sets forth Soloviev's call to recognize the universal fatherhood of the successors of St. Peter.

The purpose of the following samplings is to give readers a preview of the richness of Soloviev's thought.

Soloviev begins with an incisive history of the Eastern heresies of the fourth to ninth centuries. Stressing the intimate relationship between those heresies and the policies of the Byzantine Empire, he delineates the connections among those heresies. He emphasizes the inevitability of conflict between the Byzantine Empire and the papacy in this period. Readers will want to ponder his reasons for asserting that "Islam is simply sincere and logical Byzantinism, free from all its inner contradictions."

In part one, Soloviev underlines the fact that prior to the schism, leaders of the Eastern churches repeatedly appealed to Rome to rescue them from heresies and encroachments of the Byzantine emperors. And always, he reminds us, Rome ensured the ultimate triumph of truth. Therefore, he claims, the Eastern schism cannot be justified. The early ecumenical councils (especially the fourth, at Chalcedon in 451), to which the separated Eastern churches firmly adhere, clearly recognized the universal jurisdiction and authority of Rome. No council accepted by the Eastern churches ever condemned Rome. Moreover, since the break between East and West, those churches have been unable on their own to convoke an ecumenical council.

Soloviev's defense of the papacy begins negatively in part two with his critique of the Russian Orthodox church (and therefore of all the Eastern churches) separated from Rome. The unity of the separated Eastern churches is "based on a broad but hollow indifference, implying no organic bond and requiring no effective fellowship between particular churches." Indeed, in Eastern Orthodoxy the universal Church is only a "logical concept." The parts, that is, the particular churches, "are real, but the whole of it is nothing but a subjective abstraction."

The issue of caesaropapism (control of the Church by the secular power) looms large in Soloviev's evaluation of the separated Eastern churches. It is practically inevitable, he argues, that individual national, ethnic churches will come under the power of the state. Soloviev illustrates this at length from the history of the Russian church, whose experience in this regard is typical of all the Eastern Orthodox churches. The only way in which a national church can avoid being subject to the authority of the ruling power is to have "a real *point d'appui* [point of support] outside the confines of state and nation." One of the functions of the papacy is to provide that support. In 1872 the Bulgarian Orthodox church was condemned by a council of prelates of other Eastern Orthodox churches for the heresy of "phyletism," which means a tendency to let racial and national divisions control the church's life. Soloviev declares that what was seen as heresy among the

Bulgarians is accepted as orthodox in all the other Eastern Orthodox churches.

Soloviev points to the logic of protest, and makes a demand of Eastern opponents of the papacy. They must offer some alternative, positive principle of authority. He notes that Eastern anti-papal apologists insist on conciliarism as the appropriate form of church structure. For them, ecumenical councils constitute the ultimate authority in matters of doctrine. But Soloviev scoffs at this. The East has never convoked and still cannot convoke an ecumenical council. (He could have added that no ecumenical council has decreed that ecumenical councils are the final authority for the Church.) In fact, he says, if the universal Church is properly conciliar in structure, then the Eastern Orthodox do not have either "a true church constitution or a regular church government," because they cannot summon an ecumenical council.

The conciliarism advocated by Eastern Orthodox apologists is incomplete, according to Soloviev. Jesus Christ himself did give a conciliar structure to the Church, founded on the council of apostles. But to maintain harmony within the council and among his followers down through the ages, he established the papacy as the center and guarantor of unity.

Though the whole of this abridgment constitutes an apologia for the papacy, Soloviev concentrates on his case for the papacy in part three. He contends that the Church is the necessary instrument by which Christ seeks to bring the human race into the kingdom of God. Christ affirmed this mission in his high-priestly prayer at the Last Supper. He willed "to provide an actual organic basis for this work by founding his visible Church and by giving it a single head in the person of Peter as the guarantee of its unity." In other words, Christ established papal authority and infallibility to preserve his Church from worldly limits, such as nationalism. Only those persons who submit to the Church's authority and to the truth she proclaims can know true freedom. Only in that way can they be assured they are submitting to Christ on his own terms, not on theirs.

To attract the attention of his fellow Orthodox, Soloviev some-times teases them about their self-perception. The end toward which we all are striving, he reminds them, is union with God and with one another. Each of the main Christian traditions has a different method of reaching that goal. Catholics, explains Soloviev, think the voyage should be undertaken in a large, seaworthy vessel, fully equipped, with the finest of navigators. Protestants, on the other hand, think that each person should build his own little boat and travel alone, so that he will have greater freedom. And what about the Orthodox? They hold that the best way to reach harbor "is to pretend that you are there already," and that you therefore have a great advantage over your brothers in the West.

In many ways Soloviev challenges the Eastern Orthodox Christians. He repeatedly insists that an international center of unity is essential to the Church's life. Christ has foreseen this need and provided for it in the office of the papacy. He asks Eastern apologists this question: If (as you assert) the universal Church (which you claim to be) can proclaim the truth of Christ apart from the office of Peter, how do you explain the fact that the Eastern bishops, successors to the apostles, have been silent for a thousand years? Or, dares Soloviev, let us see you convoke a council with no support from Peter's successor, a council which you yourselves would regard as ecumenical.

Repeatedly, Soloviev pleads with his fellow Eastern Christians to be reconciled to Rome. "Whatever is holy and sacred for us [the Russian Orthodox] is also holy and sacred for them [the Catholics]." He emphasizes the fact that the separated churches of the East hold much the same faith as does Rome. The essentially contemplative nature of Eastern piety and the more active piety of the West are complementary, he argues, and therefore should be unitive, not divisive, forces. Reunion with Rome would not require the Eastern churches to give up their unique heritage. Rather, it would restore to them their "catholic or universal character."

With regard to the relationship of East and West, Soloviev's basic conviction is that the separated Eastern churches and the

Catholic Church are essentially one. They are separated de facto but not de jure. In one of his letters, Soloviev reveals that on the state census he identified his religion as "Orthodox-Catholic."[4] He would be sympathetic to Aidan Nichols' contention that the Orthodox churches are in a state of "partial schism."[5] Nichols refers us to *Unitatis Redintegratio* of Vatican II (15). The council acknowledged that these churches have preserved the apostolic succession and therefore have valid sacraments. It went on to teach that "through the celebration of the Eucharist of the Lord in each of these churches, the Church of God is built up and grows in stature. . . ."[6] In other words, says Nichols, "in the Eucharist of the Eastern churches the one Church itself is present and is edified. So the Church which the Catholic Church uniquely is . . . *comes to be more fully precisely through the eucharistic life of these dissident churches.*"[7]

It is clear Catholic teaching that any church not in communion with the bishop of Rome is in schism. Nichols insists it should also be clear that to the extent that Eastern Orthodox celebrations build up the one Church of Jesus Christ (as Vatican II asserts), those churches are not in schism. Hence his concept of "partial schism."

In part four, Soloviev introduces a theme seldom mentioned in Catholic apologetics. The particular churches (dioceses, provinces, patriarchates) constitute the universal Church, whose unity must be expressed in "a higher unit." Widening the focus of his thought, Soloviev insists that if all the spiritual families which constitute mankind are to be brought into one family, they must be under a common fatherhood. (Recall that Vatican II's *Lumen*

---

[4] Robert F. Slesinski, "V. S. Solovyov: The Centenary of a Death," *Communio* 26, Winter 1999, 786.

[5] Aidan Nichols, O.P., *Rome and the Eastern Churches: A Study in Schism* (Collegeville: The Liturgical Press, 1992), 25.

[6] Pope John Paul II recalls this teaching in *Ut Unum Sint* (1995), 50.

[7] Nichols, 19 (emphasis added).

Gentium 1 speaks of the Catholic Church as the sacrament of the unity of mankind.) Christ founded not particular churches, but the universal Church. That Church "he entrusted to Peter as the one supreme representative of the divine fatherhood to the whole family of the sons of man."

Earlier we noted that Florovsky, the leading Russian Orthodox ecumenist of the last century, credits Soloviev with a "momentous" contribution to the discussion of Christian unity. Yet, strangely, in his essay Florovsky does not specify that contribution or what he calls Soloviev's "true legacy." He gives no hint of Soloviev's central thesis that the Russian church (and all the other separated churches of the East) must be reconciled to Rome in order to be truly Catholic. Florovsky simply dismisses what he calls Soloviev's "Romanism," saying it has nothing to do with the man's "true legacy." As an unwilling beneficiary, Florovsky can choose not to accept his share of Soloviev's legacy. But Soloviev's "true legacy" which Florovsky calls "momentous" is precisely the "Romanism" which Florovsky rejects.

Soloviev's "true legacy" consists of three simple propositions. The universal jurisdiction and infallible teaching authority of the papacy were instituted by Jesus Christ as a perpetual gift to his Church. Apart from the papacy, the Eastern churches will always remain what they are now, ethnic, national churches, totally independent and disunited. Only in union with Rome can the separated Eastern churches become truly Catholic.

Seldom, if ever, has this Catholic doctrine of the Church been stated more eloquently, more persuasively in an apologetic context than by Vladimir Soloviev.

Requiescat in pace.

—Fr. Ray Ryland

PART ONE

The Papacy and Six
Centuries of Eastern Heresies

T HE BYZANTINE transformation of the Roman Empire, begun by Constantine the Great, continued by Theodosius, and finally achieved by Justinian, produced no more than a nominally Christian state. Its laws, its institutions, and a good deal of its public morality all retained unmistakable characteristics of the old paganism. Slavery continued to be legal; and crimes, especially political misdemeanors, were punished by law with an exquisite cruelty. This contrast between professed Christianity and practical savagery is aptly personified in the founder of the Second Empire: Constantine believed sincerely in the Christian God, paid honor to the bishops, and discussed the Trinity with them; yet he had no scruple about exercising the right of a pagan husband and father, putting Fausta and Crispus to death.

So glaring a contradiction between faith and life, however, could not last long without some attempt at reconciliation. Rather than sacrifice its actual paganism, the Byzantine Empire attempted in self-justification to pervert the purity of the Christian idea. This compromise between truth and error lies at the heart of all those heresies (often devised by the imperial power and always, except in certain individual instances, favored by it) which distracted Christendom from the fourth century to the ninth.

The fundamental truth and distinctive idea of Christianity is the perfect union of the divine and the human individually achieved in Christ, and finding its social realization in Christian humanity, in which the divine is represented by the Church, centered in the supreme pontiff, and the human by the state. This intimate relation between Church and state implies the primacy of the former, since the divine is previous in time and superior in being to the human. Heresy attacked the perfect unity of the divine and the human in Jesus Christ precisely in order to undermine the living bond between Church and state, and to confer upon the latter an absolute independence. Hence it is clear why the emperors of the Eastern Empire, intent on maintaining within Christendom the absolutism of the pagan state, were so partial to all the heresies, which were but manifold variations on a single theme:

Jesus Christ is not the true Son of God, consubstantial with the

Father; God has not become incarnate; nature and mankind remain cut off from divinity and are not united to it; consequently, the human state may rightly keep its independence and supremacy intact. Constantius and Valens had indeed good reason to support Arianism.

The humanity of Jesus Christ constitutes a person complete in itself, and is united to the Word of God only by a relationship. From this follows the practical conclusion that the human state is a complete and absolute entity, acknowledging no more than an external relationship to religion. This is the essence of the Nestorian heresy, and it becomes clear why on its appearance the Emperor Theodosius II took it under his protection and did all he could to uphold it.

The humanity in Jesus Christ is absorbed by his divinity: here is a heresy apparently the exact opposite of the preceding. It is nothing of the sort, however. If the premise is different, the conclusion is exactly the same. If Christ's human nature exists no longer, the Incarnation is simply a past event; nature and mankind remain utterly outside the sphere of the divine. Christ has borne away to heaven all that was his and has abandoned the earth to Caesar. It was an unerring instinct which moved the same Theodosius, regardless of the apparent inconsistency, to transfer his favor from vanquished Nestorianism to the newborn Monophysitism, and to bring about its formal adoption by a quasi-ecumenical council, the "robber-council" of Ephesus.

And even after the authority of a great Pope had prevailed over that of a heretical council, the emperors, more or less abetted by the Greek hierarchy, did not cease to attempt fresh compromises. The *Henoticon*[1] of the Emperor Zeno (which caused the first prolonged rupture between East and West, the schism of Acacius[2])

---

[1] A heretical document, A.D. 482, that sought to reconcile Catholics and Monophysites.—ED.

[2] Schism between Constantinople and Rome (484–519) that began with Pope Felix III's excommunication of Constantinopolitan Patriarch Acacius, his accomplices, and his followers.—ED.

and the unprincipled intrigues of Justinian and Theodora were followed by a new imperial heresy. Monothelitism maintained that there is no human will or activity in the God-Man, that his human nature is purely passive, entirely controlled by the absolute fact of his divinity. This was, in effect, to deny human freedom and energy; it was that fatalism or quietism which would give human nature no share in the working out of its own salvation; for it is God alone who operates, and the whole duty of the Christian consists in passive submission to the divine fact, represented in its spiritual aspect by the unchanging Church and in its temporal aspect by the sacred power of the god Caesar. Maintained for more than fifty years by the empire and the whole Eastern hierarchy, with the exception of a few monks who had to seek refuge in Rome, the Monothelite heresy was condemned at Constantinople in 680, only to make room before long for a new imperial compromise between Christian truth and the spirit of Antichrist.

The intimate union of the Creator and the creature is not confined in Christian belief to the rational being of man; it includes also his corporeal being and, through the latter, the material nature of the whole universe. In their compromise, the heretics first of all tried in vain to abstract in principle the very *substance* of man's being from the divine-human unity, at one time by declaring it absolutely separate from the divinity (in Nestorianism), at another by making it vanish completely into the divine (in Monophysitism); second, they tried to abstract human will and activity, the *rational being* of man, by absorbing it into the divine operation (in Monothelitism); there only remained, third, the *corporeal nature*, the external being of man and, through him, of the whole of nature. The denial to the material and sensible world of all possibility of redemption, sanctification, and union with God is at the root of the Iconoclastic heresy.

The Resurrection of Jesus Christ in the flesh has proved that bodily existence is not excluded from the union of the human and the divine, and that external and sensible objectivity can and must become the real instrument and visible image of the divine power. Hence the cult of holy images and relics, hence the legitimate belief in material miracles wrought by these sacred objects. Thus in declaring war on these images, the Byzantine emperors were not attacking a religious custom or a mere detail of worship so much as a necessary and infinitely important application of Christian truth itself. To claim that divinity cannot be sensibly expressed or externally manifested, or that the divine power cannot employ visible and symbolic means of action, is to rob the divine Incarnation of all its reality. It was more than a compromise; it was the suppression of Christianity.

Just as a grave social and political issue lay hidden under the semblance of a purely theological dispute in the previous heresies, so the Iconoclastic movement, under the guise of a ritual reformation, threatened to shatter the social organism of Christendom. The material realization of the divine, signified in the sphere of religious worship by holy images and relics, is represented in the social sphere by an institution. There is in the Christian Church a materially fixed point, an external and visible center of action, an image and an instrument of the divine power. The Apostolic See of Rome, that miraculous icon of universal Christianity, was directly involved in the Iconoclastic struggle, since all the heresies were, in the final analysis, denials of the reality of that divine Incarnation, and Rome represented its permanence in the social and political order.

It is indeed historically evident that all the heresies actively supported or passively accepted by the majority of the Greek clergy encountered insuperable opposition from the Roman Church and finally came to grief on this rock of the gospel. This is especially true of the Iconoclastic heresy; for in denying all external manifestation of the divine in the world it made a direct attack on the raison d'être of the Chair of St. Peter as the real objective center of the visible Church.

The pseudo-Christian empire of Byzantium was bound to engage in decisive combat with the orthodox papacy; for the latter was not only the infallible guardian of Christian truth but also the first realization of that truth in the collective life of the human race. To read the moving letters of Pope Gregory II to the barbarous Isaurian emperor is to realize that the very existence of Christianity was at stake. The outcome of the struggle could not be in doubt; the last of the imperial heresies went the way of its predecessors and finally closed the circle of theoretic or dogmatic compromises which Constantine's successors had attempted between Christian truth and the principle of paganism. The era of imperial heresies was followed by the emergence of Byzantine "Orthodoxy." To understand this fresh phase of the anti-Christian spirit, we must revert to its origins in the preceding period.

Throughout the history of the great Eastern heresies, extending over five centuries from the time of Arius to that of the last Iconoclasts, we constantly find in the empire and Church of the East three main parties whose alternating victories and defeats form the framework of this curious evolution.

We see in the first place the champions of formal heresy, regularly instigated and supported by the imperial court. From the religious point of view, they represented the reaction of Eastern paganism to Christian truth; politically, they were the declared enemies of that independent ecclesiastical government founded by Jesus Christ and represented by the Apostolic See of Rome. They began by conceding to Caesar, whose protégés they were, unbounded authority not only in the government of the Church but even in matters of doctrine; and when Caesar, impelled by the orthodox majority of his subjects and by the fear of playing into the hands of the pope, ended by betraying his own dependents, the leaders of the heretical party sought more solid support elsewhere by exploiting the separatist and semipagan tendencies of the various nations which were free, or were aiming at freedom, from the Roman yoke. Thus Arianism, the religion of the empire under Constantius and Valens but abandoned by their successors, claimed the allegiance of the Goths and Lombards for centuries; Nestorianism, betrayed by its champion Theodosius II, was for a time welcomed by the Eastern Syrians; and Monophysitism, thrust out from Byzantium in spite of all the efforts of the emperors, finally became the national religion of Egypt, Abyssinia, and Armenia.

At the opposite extreme to this heretical party, triply anti-Christian—in its religious doctrine, its secularism, and its nationalism—we find the absolutely orthodox Catholic party engaged in defending the purity of the Christian idea against all the pagan compromises and in championing free and worldwide ecclesiastical government against the onslaughts of caesaropapism and the aims of national separatism. This party could not count on the favor of earthly powers; of the higher clergy it included only individuals here and there. But it relied on the greatest religious force of those times, the monks, as well as on the simple faith of the mass of devout believers, at least in the central parts of the Byzantine Empire. Moreover, these orthodox Catholics found and recognized in the central Chair of Peter the mighty palladium of religious truth and freedom. To indicate the moral weight and ecclesiastical importance of this party, it is enough to say that it was the party of St. Athanasius the Great, of St. John Chrysostom, of St. Flavian, of St. Maximus the Confessor, and of St. Theodore of the Studium.

It was neither the declared heretics nor the genuinely orthodox, however, who controlled the destinies of the Christian East for many centuries. The decisive role in the story was played by a third party which, although it occupied an intermediate position between the other two, was distinguished from them by more than mere verbal subtleties; it had a clearly defined aim and pursued a well-considered policy. The great majority of the higher Greek clergy belonged to this party, which we may call semi-orthodox or, rather, "orthodox anti-Catholic." These priests held firmly to orthodox dogma, either from theoretical conviction or from force of habit or from devotion to the common tradition. They had nothing in principle against the unity of the universal Church, provided only that the center of that unity was situated in their midst; and since in point of fact this center was situated elsewhere, they preferred to be Greeks rather than Christians, and accepted a divided Church rather than the Church unified by a power which was, in their eyes, foreign and hostile to their nationality. As Christians, they could not be caesaropapists in principle, but as patriotic Greeks first and foremost, they preferred the Byzantine caesaropapism to the Roman papacy.

Unluckily for them, the Greek autocrats distinguished themselves for the most part as the champions or even as the authors of heresy; and what they found still more intolerable was that the rare occasions when the emperors took orthodoxy under their protection were exactly the occasions when the empire and the papacy were in accord with one another. To disturb this accord and to attach the emperors to orthodoxy while weaning them from Catholicism was the chief aim of the Greek hierarchy. In pursuit of this aim they were ready, despite their sincere orthodoxy, to make sacrifices even on questions of dogma.

These pious gentlemen regarded formal and explicit heresy with horror, but when it pleased the divine Caesar to offer them his own version of orthodox dogma, they did not scrutinize it too closely. They preferred to receive a revised or incomplete formula at the hands of a Greek emperor rather than accept the truth pure and intact from the mouth of a pope; they were glad to see Zeno's *Henoticon* replace the dogmatic epistle of St. Leo the Great.

In the six or seven successive episodes in the history of the Eastern heresies, the policy of the pseudo-orthodox party was always the same. When heresy in its first flush of victory was being thrust upon them with violence, these prudent people, having a pronounced distaste for martyrdom, gave way, though unwillingly. Thanks to their passive support, the heretics were able to convene general assemblies as large as, or even larger than, the true ecumenical councils. But when the blood of confessors, the fidelity of the mass of the people, and the threatening authority of the Roman pontiff had compelled the imperial power to forsake the cause of error, these unwilling heretics returned en masse to orthodoxy and, like the laborers hired at the eleventh hour, received their full pay.

The heroic confessors seldom survived the persecutions, and it was the worldly-wise who enjoyed the victory of truth. They formed the majority in the orthodox councils, as they had previously in the heretical conventions; and though they could not refuse concurrence to the pope's representatives when he sent them a precise and definite formulation of orthodox dogma (though at first they even expressed their concurrence with more or less sincere enthusiasm), the evident triumph of the papacy soon brought them back to their prevailing sentiment of jealous hatred toward the Apostolic See, and they proceeded to use all the efforts of a determined will and all the resources of an astute intelligence to counterbalance the success of the papacy, to rob it of its rightful influence, and to set up in opposition to it an unreal and usurped authority. The pope had been useful in dealing with heresy; but once heresy was done with, what need was there of the pope? Could not the patriarch of the old Rome be replaced by the patriarch of the new?

Thus each triumph of orthodoxy, which was always the triumph of the papacy, was invariably followed at Byzantium by an anti-Catholic reaction into which the sincere but shortsighted champions of orthodoxy were also drawn. This separatist reaction would last until a new heresy, more or less favored by the imperial power, supervened to disturb orthodox consciences and remind them of the advantage of a genuine ecclesiastical authority.

When official Arianism, having reigned supreme in the Eastern Empire for half a century, failed in the attempt to invade the Western Church, and a Spaniard came to Constantinople with the blessing of the Roman and Milanese pontiffs to restore orthodoxy there, the decisive part played by the papacy in the great struggle and in the final triumph of the true doctrine of the Trinity did not fail to arouse the jealousy of those prudent members of the Greek hierarchy who, having been semi-Arians under Constantius and Valens, had now become completely orthodox under Theodosius. Gathered in the year 380 in an assembly which a great saint of the period, Gregory the Theologian, has described in familiar words, they constituted themselves an ecumenical council without more ado, as though the whole of Western Christendom did not exist; they wantonly replaced the Nicene Profession of Faith, the common standard of universal orthodoxy in East and West, with a new formula of purely Eastern origin, and they crowned their uncanonical proceedings by conferring on the bishop of Constantinople, a mere suffragan of the archbishop of Heraclea, the dignity of first patriarch of the Eastern church, in spite of the apostolic Sees of Alexandria and Antioch which the great Nicene council had confirmed in their rights.

If the sovereign pontiffs had been ordinarily as ambitious as some like to represent them, if, indeed, the defense of their lawful rights had been dearer to their hearts than the preservation of universal peace, nothing could have prevented the separation of the two churches in the year 381. But the generosity and Christian spirit of Pope Damasus succeeded in averting that disaster. He recognized that the Creed of Constantinople was as orthodox as that of Nicaea and that the additional article on the Holy Spirit was justified in view of the new heresy of the Pneumatomachi, who held the Third Person of the Trinity to be a creature begotten by the Son, thus denying the procession of the Spirit from the Father. The Pope therefore approved the dogmatic act of the Greek council in his own name and in that of the whole Latin Church, and thereby gave it the authority of a true ecumenical council; the usurpation of the patriarchate by the See of Constantinople was ignored.

But the papacy played an even greater part in the history of the chief Christological heresies during the fifth century than in the Arian struggles of the fourth. Most of the Greek bishops, forming our third party, were shamefully compromised by their passive acquiescence in the "robber-council" of Ephesus at which the great body of orthodox prelates were obliged not only to see Flavian done to death before their eyes, but also to sign a heretical profession of faith. In contrast to this criminal weakness, the papacy appeared in all its moral power and majesty in the person of St. Leo the Great. At Chalcedon, the great number of Greek bishops who had taken part in Dioscorus' "robber-council" were obliged to beg forgiveness of the legates of Pope Leo, who was hailed as the divinely inspired head of the universal Church. Such homage to justice and truth was too much for the moral mediocrity of these corrupt prelates. The anti-Catholic reaction followed immediately at the very same council.

After enthusiastically applauding the Pope's dogmatic epistle as "the very words of the blessed apostle Peter," the Byzantine bishops attempted to substitute for this apostolic utterance an ambiguous formula which left the door open to heresy. Foiled in this attempt, they chose a different ground for their anti-Catholic activities, and in an irregular session of the council they asserted the imperial patriarch's primacy of jurisdiction over the whole East, and his equality with the pope. This act, aimed against the sovereign pontiff, had nevertheless to be humbly submitted by the Greeks for the ratification of the Pope himself, who quashed it completely. Thus, in spite of all, the Council of Chalcedon has its place in history as an outstanding triumph for the papacy. But the orthodox anti-Catholics could not rest content with such an outcome, and this time the reaction was decisive and persistent. Pure orthodoxy being too Roman for them, they began to flirt with heresy.

The Patriarch Acacius favored the Emperor Zeno's *Henoticon*, which was a compromise with Monophysitism. The Pope excommunicated Acacius, who has the unhappy distinction of giving his name to the first formal schism between East and West. The main circumstances of this anti-Catholic reaction, however, prevented its development into a definite cleavage. In the schism of Acacius, the semi-orthodox party was discredited by the concessions its members had to make to undisguised heresy, concessions which not only did violence to the religious convictions of the faithful but did nothing to meet the demands of the heretics. The latter, emboldened by the *Henoticon* which they had rejected with contempt, proceeded to set the whole of Egypt ablaze and threatened to separate it from the empire. On the other side, the orthodox monks, exasperated by the treachery of the prelates, were stirring up discord in Syria and Asia Minor; and even in Constantinople itself, the crowd applauded the monk who pinned the Pope's bull of excommunication to the cope of the schismatic patriarch.

To prolong such a state of affairs was not good policy; urged by the imperial government, the successors of Acacius showed themselves more and more conciliatory. At length, under the Emperor Justin I, peace was concluded between the churches to the advantage and honor of the papacy. The Eastern bishops, in order to prove their orthodoxy and gain admission to the communion of the Roman Church, were obliged to accept and sign without reservation the dogmatic formula of Pope Hormisdas, that is, to recognize implicitly the supreme doctrinal authority of the Apostolic See.[3] But the submission of the Greek prelates was not sincere; they were still mediating an entente with the Monophysites against the See of Peter. Despite their underhanded intrigues, however, the power of the papacy was demonstrated afresh —as the liturgical books of the Greco-Russian church record— when Pope St. Agapitus, who had come to Constantinople on a political mission, deposed on his own personal authority a patriarch suspected of Monophysitism, set up an orthodox patriarch in his place, and compelled all the Greek bishops to sign anew the formula of Hormisdas.

Meanwhile, Justinian's forces were victorious in Africa and Italy, Rome was recovered from the Ostrogoths, and the pope was once again de facto the subject of the Byzantine emperor. In these circumstances and under the influence of his wife's Monophysite tendencies, Justinian changed his attitude toward the head of the Church. The anti-Catholic party seized the reins and Pope Vigilius, a prisoner at Constantinople, was destined to bear the brunt of a triumphant reaction. The supreme teacher of the Church maintained his own orthodoxy, but as sovereign head of the government of the Church he found himself deeply humiliated; and soon afterward, a bishop of Constantinople thought himself powerful enough to usurp the title of ecumenical patriarch.

---

[3] John, the patriarch of Constantinople, wrote to the Pope: "*Prima salus est quia in sede apostolica inviolabilis semper catholica custoditur religio*" ["It is first of all clear that the Catholic religion is guarded inviolate in the Apostolic See"] (Labbe, *Concil.*, 8:451:2).

This bishop, orthodox in his doctrine and an exemplary ascetic in his private life, fulfilled the ideal of the great anti-Catholic party. But a new imperial whim was sufficient to dispel the illusion of this precarious orthodoxy. The Emperor Heraclius thought he saw in Monothelitism the means of reuniting the orthodox with the moderate Monophysites, thus restoring peace to the empire, consolidating the Greek religion, and freeing it once and for all from the influence of Rome.

The higher clergy throughout the East welcomed this idea unreservedly. The patriarchal sees were occupied intermittently by a series of more or less fanatical heretics, and Monothelitism became for half a century the official religion of the whole Greek Empire as semi-Arianism had been in the time of Constantius. A few monks, the heroic champions of orthodoxy, headed by St. Maximus the Confessor, took refuge in Rome; and once again the apostle Peter strengthened his brethren.

A long succession of popes from Severinus to St. Agatho met the heresies of the emperors with an unflinching opposition, and one of them, St. Martin, was dragged by soldiers from the altar, was haled like a criminal from Rome to Constantinople and from Constantinople to the Crimea, and finally gave his life for the orthodox faith. At length, after fifty years' struggle, religious truth and moral power won the day. The mighty empire and its worldly clergy surrendered once again to a poor, defenseless pontiff.

At the Council of Constantinople, the sixth ecumenical council, the Apostolic See of Rome was honored as an authority that had remained untainted by error; and the Greek bishops received Pope Agatho's pronouncement with a repetition of the acclamations with which the fathers of Chalcedon had formerly hailed Leo the Great. But once again it was not long before a powerful reaction followed this momentary enthusiasm. While the true heroes of orthodoxy, such as Maximus the Confessor, could not find words strong enough to extol the preeminence and achievements of the Roman See, the orthodox anti-Catholics, though profiting by its achievements, were too jealous of its preeminence to give it recognition. In their humiliation and irritation at the long list of heretics and heresiarchs who had defiled the See of Constantinople and whom the council was bound to anathematize, the Greek bishops found revenge by inventing the heresy of Pope Honorius and foisting it upon the good-natured Roman legates.

Not content with this, they reassembled some years after the council in the imperial palace at Constantinople (*in Trullo*). They claimed ecumenical authority for this gathering on various absurd pretexts: either by representing it, contrary to the evidence, as the continuation of the sixth council or, alternatively—such is the usual duplicity of falsehood—by reckoning it as the conclusion of the fifth and sixth councils under the outlandish title of "Quinisext." The object of these absurd deceptions came out clearly in certain canons promulgated by the fathers of the Trullan council, which condemned various disciplinary and ritual usages of the Roman Church. There, ready-made, were the grounds for schism; and if schism did not follow then and there, two centuries before Photius, we have only to thank the Iconoclast emperor, Leo the Isaurian, who at that moment came on the scene to upset the well-laid plans of the orthodox anti-Catholics.

Here was the most violent, as it was the last, of the imperial heresies; and with its emergence all the indirect and disguised denials of the Christian idea were exhausted. After the condemnation of the Iconoclasts, the fundamental dogma of Christian orthodoxy —the perfect union of the Creator and the creature—was defined in all its aspects and became an accepted fact. But the seventh ecumenical council, which achieved this task in 787, had been assembled under the auspices of Pope Adrian I and had used a dogmatic epistle of that pontiff to guide its decisions. It was again a triumph for the papacy; it could not, then, be the "Triumph of Orthodoxy." That was postponed until half a century later when, after the comparatively feeble Iconoclastic reaction brought about by the Armenian dynasty, the orthodox anti-Catholic party finally succeeded in 842 in crushing the last remnants of the imperial heresy, without the help of the pope, and in including it with all the others under a solemn anathema.[4]

---

[4] The memory of this event is perpetuated by a feast bearing the title "The Triumph of Orthodoxy," on which the anathema of the year 842 is repeated.

Indeed, Byzantine orthodoxy was positioned to triumph in 842. The great Photius, its light and glory, was already making his appearance at the court of the devout Theodora, the empress who instigated the massacre of a hundred thousand Paulician heretics. Before long, Photius would be mounting the throne of the ecumenical patriarchs.

The schism that Photius initiated in 867 and that Michael Cerularius consummated in 1054 was closely connected with the "Triumph of Orthodoxy," and was the complete realization of the ideal which the orthodox anti-Catholic party had dreamed of since the fourth century. Dogmatic truth having been now defined and all the heresies finally condemned, they had no further use for the pope; nothing remained but to crown the work by a formal separation from Rome. Furthermore, this solution suited the Byzantine emperors best; for they had come to see that it was not worthwhile rousing the religious passions of their subjects by doctrinal compromise between Christianity and paganism, thus throwing them into the arms of the papacy, when a strict theoretical orthodoxy could very well be reconciled with a political and social order which was completely pagan.

It is a significant fact, and one that has not been sufficiently investigated, that from the year 842 not a single imperial heretic or heresiarch reigned at Constantinople, and the harmony between the Greek church and state was not once seriously disturbed. The two powers had come to terms and had made their peace, bound to one another by a common idea: the denial of Christianity as a social force and as the guiding principle of historical progress. The emperors permanently embraced "Orthodoxy" as an abstract dogma, while the orthodox prelates bestowed their benediction *in saecula saeculorum* [for all time] on the paganism of Byzantine public life. And since "*sine sanguine nullum pactum*" ["without blood, no covenant"], a magnificent hecatomb of one hundred thousand Paulicians sealed the alliance of the Eastern Empire with the "Second Rome."

This "Orthodoxy" of the Byzantines was in fact nothing but ingrown heresy. The true central dogma of Christianity is the intimate and complete union of the divine and the human without confusion or division. The logical consequence of this truth— to confine ourselves to the sphere of practical human existence —is the regeneration of social and political life by the spirit of the gospel, in other words the Christianization of society and the state. Instead of this synthetic and organic union of the divine and the human, the two elements were in turn confused or divided, or one of them was absorbed or suppressed by the other.

To begin with, the divine and the human were confused in the sacred majesty of the emperor. Just as—in the confused thought of the Arians—Christ was a hybrid being, more than man and less than God, so caesaropapism, which was simply political Arianism, confused the temporal and spiritual powers without uniting them, and made the autocrat something more than the head of the state without succeeding in making him a true head of the Church.

Religious society was separated from secular society, the former being relegated to the monasteries while the forum was abandoned to pagan laws and passions. The dualism of Nestorius, condemned in theology, became the very foundation of Byzantine life. Or again, the religious ideal was reduced to bare contemplation, that is, to the absorption of the human spirit in the Godhead, an obviously Monophysite ideal. The moral life, on the other hand, was robbed of its practical force by the inculcation of the supreme ideal of passive obedience and blind submission to power; that is to say, of an ideal of quietism which was in reality the denial of human will and energy, the heresy of the Monothelites. Finally, an exaggerated asceticism attempted to suppress the bodily nature of man and to shatter the living image of the divine Incarnation—a logical though unconscious application of the Iconoclastic heresy.

This profound contradiction between professed orthodoxy and practical heresy was the Achilles' heel of the Byzantine Empire. There lay the real cause of its downfall. Indeed it deserved to fall and still more it deserved to fall before Islam. For Islam is simply sincere and logical Byzantinism, free from all its inner contradictions. It is the frank and full reaction of the spirit of the East against Christianity; it is a system in which dogma is closely related to the conditions of life and in which the belief of the individual is in perfect agreement with the social and political order.

We have seen that, in the seventh and eighth centuries, the anti-Christian movement which found expression in the imperial heresies had issued in two doctrines, of which one, that of the Monothelites, was an indirect denial of human freedom, and the other, that of the Iconoclasts, was an implied rejection of the divine phenomenality. The direct and explicit assertion of these two errors was of the essence of the Muslim religion. Islam sees in man a finite form without freedom, and in God an infinite freedom without form. God and man being thus fixed at the two opposite poles of existence, there can be no filial relationship between them; the notion of the divine coming down and taking form, or of the human ascending to a spiritual existence, is excluded; and religion is reduced to a mere external relation between the all-powerful Creator and the creature which is deprived of all freedom and owes its master nothing but a bare act of "blind surrender" (for this is what the Arabic word *islam* signifies). This act of surrender, expressed in a short formula of prayer to be invariably repeated day by day at fixed hours, sums up the whole religious background of the Eastern mind, which spoke its last word through the mouth of Muhammad.

The simplicity of this idea of religion is matched by a no less simple conception of the social and political problem: Man and the human race have no real progress to make; there is no moral regeneration for the individual and therefore, a fortiori, none for society; everything is brought down to the level of a purely natural existence; the ideal is reduced to the point at which its realization presents no difficulties. Muslim society could have no other aim but the expansion of its material power and the enjoyment of the good things of the earth. The spread of Islam by force of arms, the government of the faithful with absolute authority and according to the rules of an elementary justice laid down in the Koran—such is the whole task of the Muslim state, a task which it would be difficult not to accomplish with success.

The complete correspondence between its beliefs and its institutions gives to the whole of Muhammadan society a distinctive note of truth and sincerity which the Christian world has never been able to achieve. Christendom as a whole is certainly set upon the path of progress and transformation; and the very loftiness of its ideal forbids us to judge it finally by any one of its various phases, past or present. But Byzantinism, which was hostile in principle to Christian progress and which aimed at reducing the whole of religion to a fact of past history, a dogmatic formula, and a liturgical ceremonial—this anti-Christianity concealed beneath the mask of orthodoxy was bound to collapse in moral impotence before the open and sincere anti-Christianity of Islam.

It is interesting to observe that the new religion, with its dogma of fatalism, made its appearance at the precise moment when the Emperor Heraclius was inventing the Monothelite heresy, which was the disguised denial of human freedom and energy. It was hoped by this device to strengthen the official religion and to restore Egypt and Asia to the unity of the empire. But Egypt and Asia preferred the Arab declaration of faith to the political expedience of Byzantium. Nothing would be more astonishing than the ease and swiftness of the Muslim conquest were no account taken of the prolonged anti-Christian policy of the Eastern Empire. Five years were enough to reduce three great patriarchates of the Eastern church to the condition of historical relics. It was not a matter of conversion but simply of tearing off the mask.

History has passed judgment upon the Eastern Empire and has condemned it. Not only did it fail in its appointed task of founding the Christian state, but it strove to abort the historic work of Jesus Christ. Having attempted in vain to pervert orthodox dogma, it reduced it to a dead letter; it sought to undermine the edifice of the *Pax Christiana* [Christian peace] by attacking the central government of the universal Church; and in public life it supplanted the law of the gospel with the traditional policy of the pagan state. The Byzantines believed that true Christianity meant no more than guarding the dogmas and sacred rites of orthodoxy without troubling to Christianize social and political life; they thought it lawful and laudable to confine Christianity to the temple while they abandoned the marketplace to the principles of paganism. They had no reason to complain of the result; they were given their wish. Their dogma and their ritual were left to them; it was only the social and political power that fell into the hands of the Muslims, the rightful heirs of paganism.

The vocation to found the Christian state which the Greek Empire thus refused was transferred to the Romano-German world of the Franks and Allemanni. It was transferred to them by the only Christian power that had the right and duty to do so, by the power of Peter, the holder of the keys of the kingdom. Observe the coincidence of dates. The foundation stone of the future empire of the West was laid by the baptism and anointing of Clovis, the Frankish king, in 496, exactly when, after several fruitless attempts at agreement, it seemed that the schism of Acacius would mean the final severance of the whole of Eastern Christendom from the Catholic Church. The coincidence of the year 754 is even more remarkable: at the very moment when, with every appearance of ecumenical authority, a great Iconoclastic council at Constantinople was approving the last and most violent of the imperial heresies, directed especially against the Roman Church, Pope Stephen was anointing the father of Charlemagne at Rheims —or was it at St. Denis? Who will say?—with these words: "*Quia ideo vos Dominus per humilitatem meam mediante S. Petro unxit in reges ut per vos sua sancta exaltatur Ecclesia et princeps apostolorum suam recipiat iustitiam.*"[5]

The Carolingian dynasty was bound to the papacy by a direct filial relationship. The Pope, says an old chronicle, "*per auctoritatem apostolicam iussit Pippinum regem fieri.*"[6] This act, together with its inevitable consequences—the conquest of Italy by the Franks, the donation of Pepin, and the crowning of Charlemagne as Roman emperor—was the real and immediate cause of the separation of

[5] "Because, therefore, through my lowliness, with St. Peter mediating, the Lord has anointed you among the kings, that through you his holy Church may be exalted and the chief of the apostles receive his justice."—ED.

[6] ". . . through apostolic authority ordered Pepin to be made king."—ED.

the churches. By transferring the imperial scepter to a Western barbarian, the pope became doubly a foreigner and a foe to the Greeks. All that was needed to rob him of any support at Constantinople was that the emperors should once and for all renounce their heretical tendencies, and the union of all the "Orthodox" under the standard of anti-Catholicism would be complete. The event was not long delayed: the "Triumph of Orthodoxy" and the schism of Photius were the answer of Byzantium to the crowning of Charlemagne.

This was no matter of a dispute in theology or of a rivalry between prelates. It was simply the refusal of the old empire of Constantine to give place to the new Western power born of the close alliance of the papacy with the Frankish kingdom; everything else was secondary or by way of excuse. This view is confirmed when one recognizes that after Photius' death the schism did not take effect for a century and a half—exactly the period when Western Christendom, newly organized, seemed on the verge of collapse, when the papacy was subservient to a degenerate oligarchy and had lost its moral and religious prestige, and when the Carolingian dynasty was consumed with internal strife. But no sooner was the imperial power restored under the energetic government of the German kings, no sooner was the See of Peter again occupied by men of apostolic character, than the anti-Catholic movement at Constantinople broke forth with violence and the schism was consummated.

The Franco-German empire made sincere attempts to fulfill the task imposed upon it by its dignity as a Christian state. Notwithstanding its vices and its disorders, the new society of the West possessed one enormous advantage over the Byzantine Empire, namely, the consciousness of its own evils and a profound desire to be rid of them. Witness the innumerable councils summoned by popes, emperors, and kings to effect moral reforms in the Church and to bring the condition of society nearer to the Christian ideal. These reforms were, indeed, never fully successful, but the point is that they did occupy men's minds and that there was a refusal to accept in principle a contradiction between truth and life after the manner of the Byzantine world. The Byzantine world had never been concerned to harmonize its social conditions with its faith and had never undertaken any moral reformation. Its councils had only been interested in dogmatic formulae and in the claims of its hierarchy.

But in giving Charlemagne and Otto the Great, St. Henry and St. Louis their due, we are bound to confess that, taken all in all, the medieval monarchy (whether under the fictitious form of the Roman Empire or under the real form of a national dynasty) did not fulfill its mission as a Christian state, nor did it succeed in definitively modeling society on the Christian ideal. Those great sovereigns themselves were far from grasping the social and political problem of Christianity in all its facets, and even their ideal, for all its imperfection, proved too exalted for their successors. It was the policy of the Emperor Henry IV and of King Philip the Fair, not that of their saintly predecessors, that formed the general rule; it was their policy that paved the way for the reformation of Luther and, in time, bore fruit in the French Revolution.

The German Empire, brought to birth by the Roman See, broke the bonds of its parentage and set itself up as the rival of the papacy. Thus was taken the first and most momentous step on the path of revolution. Such rivalry between father and son could not form the organic basis of a social order. The German Empire, by exhausting its strength in an anti-Christian struggle lasting through two centuries and by attacking the very basis of Catholic unity, forfeited not only its supremacy among the nations but its very right to that supremacy. Disregarding this fictitious Roman Empire, the states of Europe themselves proceeded to constitute complete and absolutely independent units. Once again it fell to the papacy, while warding off the attacks of the German Empire, to assume the great task that the empire itself was unworthy and unable to discharge.

It is not our present concern to praise or to justify the historical achievement of a Hildebrand or an Innocent III. They have received not only vindication among historians of the present generation but encomium from such distinguished Protestant writers as Voigt, Hurter, and Neander. In what the great medieval popes achieved (beyond the purely spiritual sphere) for the culture of the European peoples, namely, the peace of nations and the good order of society, there is all the greater merit inasmuch as in this work they were fulfilling a function which did not properly belong to them.

Zoology and medicine tell us of cases in which a young and vigorous organism, accidentally injured in one of its essential elements, transfers the injured organ's function for the time being to another organ in good condition, which is known as a "vicarious organ." The imperial papacy or papal empire of Innocent III and Innocent IV was such a "vicarious organ." But this could not continue indefinitely. It needed men of exceptional quality to deal with the details of a vast and complicated political administration while keeping them all the while subordinate to the universal and spiritual goal. In succession to popes who had raised politics to the height of moral activity, there inevitably followed many more who degraded religion to the level of material interests. If Protestant historians have extolled the high achievements of the papal empire, the greatest of Catholic writers recorded its rapid decay. In immortal lines, this writer calls upon a second Charlemagne to put an end to the fatal confusion of the two powers in the Roman Church (Dante, *Inferno*, xix; *Purgatorio*, vi, xvi).

Indeed, if we consider the political and social condition of Europe toward the close of the Middle Ages, we must admit that the papacy, robbed of its secular organ and obliged to combine the two functions, was unable to give a genuinely Christian organization to the society which it had governed. International unity —the *Pax Christiana*—was nonexistent. The nations were given up to fratricidal wars, and only by supernatural intervention was the national existence of France saved.

The social constitution of Europe, based on the relationship between victors and vanquished, always retained this anti-Christian character of inequality and oppression. The predominance in public life of a pride of blood which created an insurmountable barrier between noble and serf, and of a spirit of violence which made every country the scene of civil war and plunder, in addition to a penal code so barbarous as to seem diabolically inspired—where in all this can the features of a truly Christian society be recognized?

For lack of an imperial power genuinely Christian and Catholic, the Church has not succeeded in establishing social and political justice in Europe. The nations and states of modern times, freed since the Reformation from ecclesiastical surveillance, have attempted to improve upon the work of the Church. The results of the experiment are plain to see: the idea of Christendom as a real though admittedly inadequate unity embracing all the nations of Europe has vanished. The philosophy of the revolutionaries has made praiseworthy attempts to substitute for this unity the unity of the human race—how successfully is well known: a universal militarism transforming whole nations into hostile armies and itself inspired by a national hatred such as the Middle Ages never knew; a deep and irreconcilable social conflict; a class struggle which threatens to engulf everything in fire and blood; and a continuous lessening of moral power in individuals, witnessed to by the constant increase in mental collapse, suicide, and crime—such is the sum total of the progress secularized Europe has made in the last three or four centuries.[7]

The two great historic experiments, that of the Middle Ages and that of modern times, seem to demonstrate conclusively that neither the Church—lacking the assistance of a secular power which is distinct from but responsible to her—nor the secular state—relying upon its own resources—can succeed in establishing Christian justice and peace on earth. The close alliance and

---

[7] I am speaking here of the general result; that there has been progress in certain directions is unquestionable. We need only mention the mitigation of the severity of penal legislation and the abolition of torture. The gain is considerable, but can it be regarded as secure? If class war were to break out again one day with all the fury of a long-restrained hatred, we should witness remarkable happenings. Events of ill omen, acts of Mezentian barbarity, have already taken place between Paris and Versailles in 1871.

organic union of the two powers *without confusion and without division* is the indispensable condition of true social progress.

~

As a member of the true and venerable Eastern or Greco-Russian Orthodox church, which speaks neither through an anti-canonical synod nor through the employees of the secular power, but through the utterance of her great Fathers and Doctors, I recognize as supreme judge in matters of religion him who has been recognized as such by St. Irenaeus, St. Dionysius the Great, St. Athanasius the Great, St. John Chrysostom, St. Cyril, St. Flavian, the Blessed Theodoret, St. Maximus the Confessor, St. Theodore of the Studium, St. Ignatius, and on and on—namely, the apostle Peter, who lives in his successors and who has not heard our Lord's words in vain: "You are Peter, and on this rock I will build my church" (Matt. 16:18); "Strengthen your brethren" (Luke 22:32); "Feed my sheep, feed my lambs" (cf. John 21:15, 16, 17).

O deathless spirit of the blessed apostle, invisible minister of the Lord in the government of his visible Church, thou knowest that she has need of an earthly body for her manifestation. Twice already hast thou embodied her in human society: in the Greco-Roman world, and again in the Romano-German world; thou hast made both the empire of Constantine and the empire of Charlemagne to serve her. After these two provisional incarnations she awaits her third and last incarnation. A whole world full of energies and of yearnings but with no clear consciousness of its destiny knocks at the door of universal history. What is your word, ye peoples of the Word? The multitude knows it not yet, but powerful voices issuing from your midst have already disclosed it. Two centuries ago, a Croatian priest announced it with prophetic tongue and, in our own days, a bishop of the same nation [Bishop Strossmayer] has more than once proclaimed it with superb eloquence. The utterance of the spokesmen of the Western Slavs, the great Krishanitch and the great Strossmayer, needs only a simple *amen* from the Eastern Slavs. I come to speak this *amen* in the name of a hundred million Russian Christians, in full and firm confidence that they will not repudiate me.

Your word, O peoples of the Word, is free and universal theocracy, the true solidarity of all nations and classes, the application of Christianity to public life, the Christianizing of politics; freedom for all the oppressed, protection for all the weak; social justice and good Christian peace. Open to them, therefore, thou key-bearer of Christ, and may the gate of history be for them and for the whole world the gate of the kingdom of God!

PART TWO

The State of Religion in
Russia and the Christian East

Chapter 1

The Russian Legend of St. Nicholas and St. Cassian. Its Application to the Two Separated Churches

A popular Russian legend tells how St. Nicholas and St. Cassian were once sent from Paradise upon a visit to the earth. On their journey they met a poor peasant who had got his wagon, with a load of hay upon it, stuck deep in the mud and was making fruitless efforts to get his horses on.

"Let's go and give the good fellow a hand," said St. Nicholas.

"Not I; I'm keeping out of it," replied Cassian, "I don't want to get my coat dirty."

"Well, wait for me," said Nicholas, "or go on without me if you like," and plunging without hesitation into the mud he vigorously assisted the peasant in dragging his wagon out of the rut.

When he had finished the job and caught up with his companion, he was all covered in filth; his coat was torn and soiled and looked like a beggar's rags. Peter was amazed to see him arrive at the gate of paradise in this condition.

"I say! Whoever got you into that state?" he asked.

Nicholas told his story.

"And what about you?" asked Peter, turning to Cassian. "Weren't you with him in this encounter?"

"Yes, but I don't meddle in things that are no concern of mine, and I was especially anxious not to get my beautiful clean coat dirty."

"Very well," said Peter, "you, Nicholas, because you were not afraid of getting dirty in helping your neighbor out of a difficulty, shall for the future have two feasts a year, and you shall be reckoned the greatest of saints after me by all the peasants of holy Russia. And you, Cassian, must be content with having a nice clean coat; you shall have your feast day in leap year only, once every four years."

We may well forgive Cassian for his dislike of manual labor and the mud of the highroad. But he would be quite wrong to condemn his companion for having a different idea of the duties of saints toward mankind. We may like Cassian's clean and spotless clothes, but since our wagon is still deep in the mud, Nicholas is the one we really need, the stout-hearted saint who is always ready to get to work and help us.

The Western Church, faithful to the apostolic mission, has not been afraid to plunge into the mire of history. After having been for centuries the only element of moral order and intellectual culture among the barbarous peoples of Europe, it undertook the task not only of the spiritual education of these peoples of independent spirit and uncivilized instincts but also of their material government. In devoting itself to this arduous task, the papacy—like St. Nicholas in the legend—thought not so much of the cleanliness of its own appearance as of the urgent needs of mankind. The Eastern church, on the other hand, with its solitary asceticism and its contemplative mysticism, its withdrawal from political life and from all the social problems which concern mankind as a whole, thought chiefly, like Cassian, of reaching paradise without a single stain on its clothing. The Western Church aimed at employing all its powers, divine and human, for the attainment of a universal goal; the Eastern church was only concerned with the preservation of its purity. There is the chief point of difference and the fundamental cause of the schism between the two churches.

It is a question of a different ideal of the religious life itself. The religious ideal of the separated Christian East is not false; it is incomplete. For the last thousand years in Eastern Christendom, religion has been identified with personal piety,[1] and prayer has been regarded as the one and only religious activity. The Western Church, without disparaging individual piety as the true seed of all religion, seeks the development of this seed and its blossom-

---

[1] In Old Russian, the word "piety" (*blagochestie*) was ordinarily used to express "orthodoxy," and the expression "pious belief" (*blagochestivaya vera*) was used instead of "orthodox belief."

ing into a social activity organized for the glory of God and the universal good of mankind. The Eastern prays, the Western prays and labors. Which of the two is right?

Jesus Christ founded his visible Church not merely to meditate on heaven, but also to labor upon earth and to withstand the gates of Hades. He did not send his apostles into the solitude of the desert, but into the world to conquer it and subject it to the kingdom which is not of this world, and he enjoined upon them not only the innocence of doves but also the wisdom of serpents. If it is merely a question of preserving the purity of the Christian soul, what is the purpose of all the Church's social organization and of all those sovereign and absolute powers with which Christ has armed her in giving her final authority to bind and to loose on earth as well as in heaven?

For centuries, the monks of the holy mountain of Athos, true representatives of the isolated Eastern church, have spent all their energies in prayer and the contemplation of the uncreated light of Tabor.[2] They are perfectly right: prayer and the contemplation of uncreated things are essential to the Christian life. But can we allow that this occupation of the soul constitutes the *whole* Christian life? For that is what we must do if we try to put the Orthodox East, with its peculiar character and special religious tendencies, in the place of the universal Church. We have in the East a church at prayer, but where among us is the Church in action, asserting itself as a spiritual force absolutely independent of the powers of this world? Where in the East is the Church of the living God, the Church which in every generation legislates

---

[2] By certain physiological or psychological processes which are summed up among us under the name of "cerebral action" (*umnoye delanie*), the hermits of Athos achieve a state of ecstasy in which they experience unique sensations and claim to see the divine light which manifested itself at the Transfiguration of our Lord. The curious thing is that this phenomenon is regarded as an eternal, subsistent reality. In the fourteenth century, furious controversy arose in the Greek church over the inquiry into the real nature of the light of Tabor and its relation to the essence of the Godhead.

for mankind, which establishes and develops the formulation of eternal truth with which to counteract the continually changing forms of error? Where is the Church which labors to remold the whole social life of the nations in accordance with the Christian ideal, and to guide them toward the supreme goal of Creation— free and perfect union with the Creator?

The advocates of an exclusive asceticism should remember that the perfect man spent only forty days in the wilderness; those who contemplate the light of Tabor should not forget that that light appeared only once in the earthly life of Christ, who proved by his own example that true prayer and true contemplation are simply a foundation for the life of action. If this great church, which for centuries has done nothing but pray, has not prayed in vain, she must show herself a living church, acting, struggling, victorious. But we ourselves must will that it be so.

We must above all recognize the insufficiency of our traditional religious ideal, and make a sincere attempt to realize a more complete conception of Christianity. There is no need to invent or create anything new for this purpose. We merely have to restore to our religion its catholic or universal character by recognizing our oneness with the active part of the Christian world, with the West centralized and organized for a universal activity and possessing all that we lack. We are not asked to change our nature as Easterns or to repudiate the specific character of our religious genius. We have only to recognize unreservedly the elementary truth that we of the East are but a part of the universal Church, a part moreover which has not its center within itself, and that therefore it behooves us to restore the link between our individual forces on the circumference and the great universal center which Providence has placed in the West.

There is no question of suppressing our religious and moral individuality but rather of crowning it and inspiring it with a universal and progressive life. The whole of our duty to ourselves consists simply in recognizing ourselves for what we are in reality, an organic part of the great body of Christendom, and in affirming our spiritual solidarity with our Western brethren. This moral act of justice and charity would be in itself an immense step forward on our part and the essential condition of all further advance.

Cassian need not become a different person or cease to care about keeping his clothes spotless. He must simply recognize that his comrade has certain important qualities which he himself lacks, and instead of sulking at this energetic worker he must frankly accept him as his companion and guide on the earthly voyage that still lies before them.

Chapter 2

The True Orthodoxy of the Russian People and the Pseudo-Orthodoxy of the the Anti-Catholic Theologians

The distinctively religious character of the Russian people as well as the mystical tendency exhibited in our philosophy, our literature,[1] and our arts seem to indicate for Russia a great religious mission. Moreover, when our patriots are pressed to state what it is that constitutes the supreme vocation of our country, or the Russian "idea" as it is called nowadays, they have no choice but to appeal to religion. According to them, Orthodoxy—or the religion of the Greco-Russian church, in contrast to the religious bodies of the West—constitutes the true basis of our national being. Here, to begin with, is an obvious vicious circle. If we ask how the separated Eastern church justifies its existence, we

---

[1] Our best modern writers have been impelled by a religious idealism which has proved stronger than their aesthetic vocation to abandon the too restricted sphere of literature and to appear with varying success as moralists and reformers, apostles and prophets. The untimely death of Pushkin debars us from deciding whether the religious tendency shown in his most finished productions was deep enough to become in time predominant in his thought and to make him quit the domain of pure poetry, as happened with Gogol (in *Correspondence with My Friends*), with Dostoyevsky (in *An Author's Diary*), and with Tolstoy (in *My Confession, My Religion*, etc.). It seems that the Russian genius does not discover in poetic expression its final objective or the medium suited to the embodiment of its essentially religious ideal. If Russia is called to convey her message to the world, that message must sound forth not from the dazzling regions of art and literature nor from the heights of philosophy and science, but only from the sublime and lowly peaks of religion.

are told: By having formed the Russian people and provided its spiritual nurture. And when we inquire how that people justifies its existence, the answer is: By belonging to the separated Eastern church. We are brought to this impasse by the difficulty of really deciding what we mean by this "Orthodoxy" of which we would claim the monopoly.

This difficulty does not exist for those who are really orthodox in all good conscience and in the simplicity of their hearts. When questioned intelligently about their religion, they will tell you that to be Orthodox is to be baptized a Christian, to wear a cross or some holy image on your breast, to worship Christ, to pray to the Blessed Virgin most immaculate[2] and to all the saints represented by images and relics, to rest from work on all festivals and to fast in accordance with traditional custom, to venerate the sacred office of bishops and priests, and to participate in the holy sacraments and in divine worship. That is the true Orthodoxy of the Russian people, and it is ours also.

But it is not that of our militant patriots. It is obvious that true Orthodoxy contains nothing particularist and can in no way form a national or local attribute separating us in any sense from the Western peoples; for the greater part of these peoples, the Catholic part, has precisely the same religious basis that we have. Whatever is holy and sacred for us is also holy and sacred for them. Consider this one essential point: not only is devotion to the Blessed Virgin—one of the characteristic features of Catholicism —generally practiced by Russian Orthodoxy,[3] but even special miraculous images are venerated in common by Roman Catholics and Russian Orthodox (for example, the holy Virgin of Czestochowa in Poland). If "piety" is indeed the distinctive characteris-

---

[2] "Most immaculate" or "all-immaculate" (*vseneporochnaya*) is the epithet regularly added to the name of the Blessed Virgin in our liturgical books, being the translation of the Greek *pantamomos* and other kindred words.

[3] By this term I do not exclude the "old believers" properly so-called, whose differences with the state church are not concerned with the true object of religion.

tic of our national genius, the reality that the chief emblems of that piety are common to us and the Westerns compels us to recognize our oneness with them in what we regard as the most essential thing of all.

As regards the profound contrast between the contemplative piety of the East and the active religion of the Westerns, this contrast being purely human and subjective has nothing to do with the divine objects of our faith and worship. So far from being a good reason for schism, it should rather bring the two great parts of the Christian world into a closer and mutually complementary union.

But under the influence of that evil principle which is constantly at work on earth, this difference has been abused and twisted into a division. At the moment when Russia was receiving baptism from Constantinople, the Greeks, though still in formal communion with Rome after the temporary schism of Photius,[4] were already strongly imbued with national particularism, which was fostered by the contentious spirit of the clergy, the political ambitions of the emperors, and the disputes of the theologians. The result was that the pearl of the gospel purchased by the Russian people in the person of St. Vladimir was all covered with the dust of Byzantium. The bulk of the nation was uninterested in the ambitions and hatreds of the clergy and understood nothing of the theological quibbles which were their fruit; the bulk of the nation received and preserved the essence of orthodox Christianity pure and simple, that is to say, faith and the life of religion formed by divine grace and expressed in works of piety and charity. But the

---

[4] The final rupture, which did not occur until later, in 1054, was nothing, in fact, but a mere event without any kind of legal or binding sanction. The anathema of the legates of Pope Leo IX was not aimed against the Eastern church, but solely against the person of the Patriarch Michael Cerularius and against "the partners of his folly" (folly obvious enough, to be sure); and on the other hand, the Eastern church has never been able to assemble an ecumenical council which, even according to our own theologians, is the only tribunal competent to pass judgment on our differences with the papacy.

clergy, recruited in the early days from the Greeks, and the theologians accepted the disastrous inheritance of Photius and Cerularius as an integral part of the true religion.

This pseudo-Orthodoxy of our theological schools, which has nothing in common with the faith of the universal Church or the piety of the Russian people, contains no positive element; it consists merely of arbitrary negations produced and maintained by controversial prejudice:

"God the Son does not contribute in the divine order to the procession of the Holy Spirit."

"The Blessed Virgin was not immaculate from the first moment of her existence."[5]

"Primacy of jurisdiction does not belong to the See of Rome and the pope has not the dogmatic authority of a pastor and doctor of the universal Church."

Such are the principal negations which we shall have to examine in due course. For our present purpose it is enough to observe in the first place that these negations have received no sort of religious sanction, and do not rest on any ecclesiastical authority accepted by all the Orthodox as binding and infallible. No ecumenical council has condemned or even passed judgment on the Catholic doctrines anathematized by our controversialists; and when we are offered this new kind of negative theology as the true doctrine of the universal Church, we can see in it only an extravagant imposture originating either in ignorance or in bad faith.

In the second place, it is obvious that this false Orthodoxy is no more adequate than true Orthodoxy as a positive basis for the "Russian idea." Let us try to substitute real values for this unknown quantity called "Orthodoxy" over which a pseudo-patriotic press is always working up an artificial enthusiasm. Ac-

---

[5] Thus these theologians blinded by hatred have the temerity to deny the manifest belief of the Eastern church, both Greek and Russian, which has never ceased to declare the Blessed Virgin to be all-immaculate, immaculate par excellence.

cording to you, the ideal essence of Russia is Orthodoxy, and
this Orthodoxy which you especially contrast with Catholicism
amounts in your view simply to the divergences between the two
professions of faith. The real religious basis which is common
to us and the Westerns seems to have no more than a secondary
interest for you; it is the differences between us to which you are
really attached. Very well, then, substitute these specific differences for the vague term "Orthodoxy" and declare openly that
the religious ideal of Russia consists in denying the *Filioque*, the
Immaculate Conception, and the authority of the pope.

It is the last point that you are chiefly concerned with. The others, you know well, are only pretexts; the sovereign pontiff is your
real bugbear. Essentially, all your "Orthodoxy," all your "Russian
idea" amounts to, then, is simply a national protest against the
universal power of the pope. But in the name of what?

Here begins the real difficulty of your position. This bitter
protest against the monarchy of the Church, if it is to win men's
minds and hearts, should be justified by some great positive principle. You should confront the form of theocratic government of
which you disapprove with another and better form. And that is
exactly what you cannot do. What kind of ecclesiastical constitution would you confer upon the Western peoples? Are you going to extol conciliar government and talk to them of ecumenical
councils? *Medice, cura teipsum* ["Physician, heal yourself"] (Luke
4:23). Why has not the East set up a *true* ecumenical council in
opposition to those of Trent or the Vatican? How are we to explain this helpless silence on the part of truth when faced with
the solemn self-assertion of error? Since when have the guardians
of Orthodoxy become mean-spirited curs that can only bark from
behind a wall?

In point of fact, while the great assemblies of the Church continue to fill a prominent place in the teaching and life of Catholicism, it is the Christian East which has for a thousand years been
deprived of this important feature of the universal Church, and our
best theologians, such as Philaret of Moscow, themselves admit
that an ecumenical council is impossible for the Eastern church as

long as she remains separated from the West. But it is the easiest thing in the world for our self-styled Orthodox to confront the actual councils of the Catholic Church with a council that can never take place, and to maintain their cause with weapons that they have lost and under a flag of which they have been robbed.

The papacy is a positive principle, an actual institution, and if Eastern Christians believe this principle to be false and this institution to be evil, it is for them to create the organization which they desire to see in the Church. Instead of doing so, they refer us to antiquarian traditions, though they admit that they can have no relevance to the present situation. Our anti-Catholics have good reason indeed for going so far afield in search of support for their thesis; the fact is that they dare not expose themselves to the ridicule of the whole world by declaring the Synod of St. Petersburg or the Patriarchate of Constantinople to be really representative of the universal Church. But how can they talk of appealing after all this time to ecumenical councils when they are obliged to admit that they are no longer feasible? Such beating of the air is only a complete revelation of the weakness of this anti-Catholic Orthodoxy. If the normal organization and proper constitution of the universal Church requires ecumenical councils, it is obvious that the Orthodox East, fatally deprived of this essential organ of church life, possesses no longer a true church constitution or a regular church government.

During the first three centuries of Christianity, the Church, cemented by the blood of the martyrs, convoked no worldwide councils because she had no need of them; the Eastern church of today, paralyzed and dismembered, is unable to convoke them though she feels her need of them. Thus we are placed in a dilemma: either we must admit, with our extreme sectarians, that since a certain date the Church has lost her divine character and no longer actually exists upon earth; or else, to avoid so dangerous a conclusion, we must recognize that the universal Church, having no organs of government or representation in the East, possesses them in her Western half.

This will involve the recognition of a historical truth now admitted even by the Protestants, namely, that the present-day papacy is not an arbitrary usurpation but a legitimate development of principles which were in full force before the division of the Church and against which that Church never protested. But if the papacy is recognized as a legitimate institution, what becomes of the "Russian idea" and the privilege of national Orthodoxy? If we cannot base our religious future on the official church, perhaps we can find deeper foundations for it in the Russian people.

Chapter 3

Russian Dissent. The Relative Truth of
the Raskol. Archbishop Philaret of Moscow
and His Conception of the Universal Church

If we wish to state Orthodoxy in terms of the Russian national ideal, logic compels us to seek the true expression of that ideal among our native sects and not within the domain of the official church, whose origin is Greek and whose organization, given her by Peter the Great, is Teutonic. Deprived of any specific principle or practical independence, this "Ministry of the Spiritual Affairs of the Orthodox Communion" can only reproduce the imperial clericalism of Byzantium modified by the easygoing good nature of our own people and the Teutonic bureaucracy of our administration. Apart from the particular causes which produced the *Raskol*,[1] and which have only a historical importance, it may be confidently asserted that the reason for the persistence of this schism within the nation is the obvious inadequacy of Russian church government coupled with its exaggerated pretensions.

This church, "established" by the tsar, though totally subservient to the secular power and destitute of all inner vitality, nonetheless makes use of the hierarchical idea to assume over the people an absolute authority which by right belongs only to the independent universal Church founded by Christ. The emptiness

---

[1] The generic name of *raskol* (schism) is in use among us to denote especially those of the dissenters who separated from the official church over the question of rites and who are also called *starovery* (old believers). The separation was finally consummated in the years 1666–1667, when a council assembled at Moscow anathematized the old rites.

of these claims, sensed rather than consciously recognized, has driven one section of our dissenters to fruitless attempts at constituting a Russian Orthodox church independent of the state, while another and larger section has quite frankly declared that the true Church has completely disappeared from the world since the year 1666, and that we are living under the spiritual rule of Antichrist resident at St. Petersburg.

It is plain why the advocates of the "Russian idea" take good care neither to look too closely into the *Raskol* nor to seek this elusive "idea" in that quarter. A doctrine which affirms that the Russian church and monarchy are subject to the absolute rule of Antichrist and which postpones all hope of a better state of affairs to the end of the world, obviously does not harmonize very well with an extravagant patriotism which represents Russia in her present condition as the second Israel and the chosen people of the future.

Nevertheless, it is of interest to note that it is precisely those who would have Russia undertake a religious mission all her own, namely, the Slavophils, who are compelled to ignore or to depreciate the one historical phenomenon in which the religious genius of the Russian people has shown a certain originality. On the other hand, in some of our liberal and radical "Westernizing"[2] circles, our national Protestantism, in spite of the barbarous forms it assumes, finds ready champions who imagine that they discern in it the promise of a better future for the Russian people. We ourselves, having no reason either to belittle or to overestimate this typical phenomenon of our religious history, are able to view it more objectively. We do not underrate the great part played in the rise of the *Raskol* by the profoundest ignorance, ultrademocratic tendencies, and the spirit of revolt. We shall not therefore look to it for any higher truth or any positive religious ideal. Nevertheless, we are bound to note that there has always been a spark of the divine fire in this crude and even senseless incitement of the

---

[2] This is the name (in Russian, *Zapadniki*) given to the literary party opposed to the Slavophils and attached to the principles of European civilization.

passions of the mob. There is in it a burning thirst for religious truth, a compelling need for a true and living Church.

Our national Protestantism aims its shafts at a partial and imperfect manifestation of ecclesiastical government and not at the principle of the visible Church. Even the most advanced section of our "old believers" regard an actual organized church as so necessary that, because they are robbed of it, they believe themselves to be already under the rule of Antichrist. Allowing for the ignorance which leads them to mistake Russia for the whole world, there is to be found at the bottom of all these curious errors the idea or the axiom of a church independent of the state and closely bound up with the whole intimate social life of the people—a free, powerful, and living church. And if our dissenters see the official church, whether Russian or Greek, without independence or vitality, and declare that therefore she is not the true Church of Christ, they are at least consistent in their error.

The negative truth implied in the *Raskol* remains unassailable. Neither the bloody persecutions of past generations nor the oppression of a modern bureaucracy nor the official hostility of our clergy has done anything to meet the unanswerable contention that *there exists no truly spiritual government in the Greco-Russian church.* But this is as far as the truth of our national Protestantism goes. As soon as the "old believers" abandon this simple denial and claim to have discovered some outlet for their religious instincts or to have realized their ideal of the Church, they fall into obvious contradictions and absurdities which make them an easy target for their opponents. It is not difficult for the latter to meet the *Popovtsy*[3] by proving that a religious society which has been for generations deprived of the episcopate, and which has only partly recovered this fundamental institution by entirely uncanonical proceedings, cannot be the genuine continuation of the ancient Church and the sole guardian of the Orthodox tradition. It is no more difficult

---

[3] A moderate party which by unlawful means is now in possession of a priesthood and even, since 1848, of an episcopate, whose center is at Fontana Alba in Austria.

to establish, in answer to the *Bespopovtsy*,[4] the proposition that the reign of Antichrist cannot be of indefinite length, and that logically these dissenters should repudiate not only the Church of the present day but also that of former times, which in their opinion was destroyed in the year of grace 1666. For a church against which the gates of Hades have prevailed cannot be or have been the true Church of Christ.

The great historical importance of the *Raskol* with its thousands of martyrs is the witness which it bears to the depth of religious sentiment among the Russian people and to the lively interest aroused in them by the theocratic conception of the Church. If it is, on the one hand, a matter for great joy that the majority of the populace has remained faithful to the official church (which, despite the absence of any lawful church government,[5] has at least preserved the apostolic succession and the validity of the sacraments), it would, on the other hand, have been deplorable had the entire Russian people been content with this official church such as it is; that would be a convincing proof that there was no religious future to be hoped for. The vehement and persistent protest of these millions of peasants gives us an earnest of the future regeneration of our church life. But the essentially negative character of this religious movement is a sufficient proof that the Russian people, just like every other human power left to its own resources, is incapable of realizing its highest ideal. All these aspirations and tentative movements toward a true Church indicate no more than a *passive* capacity for religion which needs an act of moral regeneration coming from a higher source than the purely national and popular element if it is to be effectively realized in a concrete, organic form.

---

[4] A small party which rejects priests and sacraments, seeing no priests as legitimate and getting by without them.

[5] All our bishops are nominated in a manner absolutely forbidden and condemned by the third canon of the seventh ecumenical council, a canon which in the eyes of our church can never have been abrogated (for lack of subsequent ecumenical councils).

We may grant that the official church ruled by a civil servant is nothing but a state institution, a minor branch of the bureaucratic administration; but the church conceived by our dissenters would at most be a merely national and democratic church. It is the idea of the universal Church which is lacking on both sides.

The article of the creed concerning the *one*, holy, *catholic*, and apostolic Church, though sung at every Mass and recited at every baptism, remains as much a dead letter for the "old Orthodox" as for the "ruling church." For the former, the church is the Russian nation—in its entirety up to the time of the Patriarch Nikon, and since his time in that section of it which has remained faithful to the old national rite. As for the theologians of the official church, their ideas on the subject are as vague as they are inconsistent. But the feature which is constant among all their variations and common to them all in spite of their differences is the absence of a positive faith in the universal Church. Here, to confine ourselves to a single writer who is worth a host of others, is the theory of the Church expounded by Archbishop Philaret, the able metropolitan of Moscow, in one of his most important works:[6]

> The true Christian Church includes all the particular churches which confess Jesus Christ "come in the flesh." The *doctrine* of all these religious societies is fundamentally the same divine truth; but it may be mingled with the opinions and errors of men. Hence there is in the *teaching* of these individual churches a distinction of greater and less purity. The doctrine of the Eastern church is purer than the rest, indeed it may be recognized as completely pure, since it does not link the divine truth to any human opinion. However, as each religious communion makes exactly the same claim to perfect purity of faith and doctrine, it does not behoove us to judge others but rather to leave the final judgment to the Spirit of God who guides the churches.

Such is the opinion of Archbishop Philaret, and the majority of the Russian clergy agree with him. The breadth and conciliatory nature of this view cannot conceal its essential defects. The

---

[6] *Conversation of an Inquirer and a Believer on the Truth of the Eastern Church.*

principle of unity and universality in the Church only extends, it would seem, to the common ground of Christian faith, namely, the dogma of the Incarnation. This truly fundamental faith in Jesus Christ, the God-Man, is not regarded as the living and fruitful seed of a further development; the theologian of Moscow would rather see in it the final unity of the Christian world and the only unity which he considers necessary. He is content to ignore the divergences that exist in the Christian religion and declares himself satisfied with the purely theoretical unity thus obtained. It is a unity based on a broad but hollow indifference, implying no organic bond and requiring no effective fellowship between particular churches. The universal Church is reduced to a logical concept. Its parts are real, but the whole of it is nothing but a subjective abstraction. Even if it has not always been thus, if the Church in her entirety was once a living body, yet that body is today a prey to death and dissolution; it is only the existence of the separate parts that is actually manifest before our eyes, while their substantial unity has vanished into the realm of the unseen world.

This idea of a "dead church" is not merely the logical conclusion which we believe to be implicit in the propositions advanced by our renowned theologian; he has labored to describe to us the universal Church as he conceived it under the form of a lifeless body made up of heterogeneous and distinct elements. He has even been inspired to apply to the Church of Christ and to the stages of its historical existence the vision of the great idol recorded in the book of Daniel. The golden head of the idol is the early Christian Church; the chest and arms of silver signify "the Church growing in strength and extent" (the age of the martyrs); the brazen stomach is "the Church in prosperity" (the triumph of Christianity and the age of the great Doctors). Finally, the Church of the present, "the Church in its divided and fragmentary condition," is represented by the two feet with their toes, in which clay is mingled with iron by the hands of men.

To accept this ill-omened symbol seriously would mean the denial of the one, infallible, and impregnable Church of God founded to last for all generations. The author perceived as much, and in subsequent editions of his work he erased the whole of this allegory; but he found nothing to put in its place. It must, however, be confessed that, in limiting the application of this symbol to the official Greco-Russian church, the distinguished representative of that institution displayed both acumen and impartiality. Iron and clay mixed by the hand of man—violence and impotence, and an artificial unity which needs only a shock to reduce it to powder: no simile could better depict the actual condition of our established church.

Chapter 4

Critical Observations on the Russian Slavophils and Their Ideas Concerning the Church

Archbishop Philaret inadvertently laid bare the real condition of the separated Eastern church. The Slavophils have attempted to conceal her nakedness under the transparent veil of an idealistic theory of the Church "in its free and living unity founded on divine grace and Christian charity." Their doctrine, insofar as it envisages the Church in general terms as a moral organism, is perfectly true, and they must be given credit for having insisted *in theory* upon its essential and indivisible unity which our official theologians and our dissenters have so completely ignored. On the other hand, those who consider that, in expounding the positive conception of the universal Church, the Slavophils confine themselves too much to vague generalizations, will find this same conception of the Church much more fully and clearly developed by certain Catholic writers, especially by the famous Möhler in his admirable work, *Die Symbolik der Christlichen Kirche.*[1]

The Church is One is the title given by Khomyakov, the leader of the Slavophil group in Russia, to a small volume of dogmatic theology which, though insignificant in itself, deserves notice as the only attempt on the part of the Slavophils to fix and systematize their theological ideas. The unity of the Church is determined by the unity of divine grace which, if it is to work within men

---

[1] *The Creed of the Christian Church.* This work is commended and frequently quoted in the *Praelectiones Theologicae* of the official dogmatic theologian of the Latin Church, the late Fr. Perrone, professor at the Collegium Romanum and member of the Society of Jesus.

and transform them into a Church of God, demands from them fidelity to a common tradition, brotherly charity, and that free consent of the individual conscience which is the definite guarantee of the truth of their faith. The Slavophils insist especially on this last point in their definition of the true Church as "the *spontaneous, inward* synthesis of unity and freedom in charity."

What objection can there be to such an ideal? Is there any Roman Catholic who—on being shown the whole of mankind or a considerable section of it inspired with divine love and brotherly charity, having but one heart and one soul and abiding thus in a free and wholly interior unity—is there, I ask, any Roman Catholic who would wish to impose upon such a society the external and binding jurisdiction of a public religious authority? Do any Roman Catholics believe that the seraphim and cherubim need a pope to govern them? And, on the other hand, is there any Protestant who, if he saw the actual attainment of final truth through "the perfection of charity," would still insist on the exercise of private judgment?

The perfectly free and inward union of men with the Godhead and with one another—that is the supreme goal, the haven toward which we steer our course. Our Western brethren are not agreed among themselves as to the best method of reaching it. Catholics believe that it is *safer to* cross the sea together in a large and seaworthy vessel built by a famous master, navigated by a skillful pilot, and equipped with all that is necessary for the voyage. Protestants, on the contrary, claim that it is for each one to construct a cockle-shell to his own liking that he may pursue his uncertain course *with greater freedom*. This latter opinion, however mistaken, is at least arguable. But what is to be said to these self-styled Orthodox who maintain that the best way of reaching harbor is to pretend that you are there already, and who think that in this respect they have the advantage over their Western brethren? The latter, it must be admitted, have never suspected that the great problem of religion is capable of so simple a solution.

The Church is one and indivisible; yet it may at the same time comprise various spheres, not to be separated but to be clearly distinguished from one another. Otherwise it would be impossible to understand the past or present history of religion or to do anything for the religious future of mankind.

Absolute perfection can only belong to that higher part of the Church which has already once for all appropriated and assimilated the fullness of divine grace—the Church triumphant or the realm of glory. Midway between this divine sphere and the purely earthly elements of visible humanity stands the divine-human organism of the Church, invisible in its mystical power and visible in its present manifestation, sharing equally in the perfection of heaven and in the conditions of material existence. This is the Church, properly speaking, and it is with her that we are concerned. She is not perfect in the absolute sense, but she must possess all the necessary means of secure progress toward the supreme ideal—the perfect unity of the whole of creation in God—in spite of countless obstacles and difficulties, through the struggles, temptations, and weaknesses of men.

Here below, the Church does not have the perfect unity of the heavenly kingdom. Nevertheless, she must have a certain real unity, a bond at once organic and spiritual which constitutes her a concrete institution, a living body, and a moral individual. Though she does not include the whole of mankind in an actual material sense, she is nevertheless *universal* insofar as she cannot be confined exclusively to any one nation or group of nations, but must have an international center from which to spread throughout the whole universe.

The Church here below, though she is founded on the revelation of God and is the guardian of the deposit of faith, does not therefore enjoy absolute and immediate knowledge of all truths; but she is *infallible*, that is to say, she cannot be mistaken when at a given moment she defines such-and-such a religious or moral truth, the explicit knowledge of which has become necessary to her. The Church on earth is not absolutely free, since she is subject to the conditions of finite existence; but she must be sufficiently *independent* to be able to carry on a constant and active struggle against the powers of the enemy and to prevent the gates of Hades from prevailing against her.

Such is the true Church on earth, the Church which in spite of the imperfection of her human element has received from God the right, the power, and all the required means to raise and guide mankind toward its appointed end. Were she not one and universal, she could not serve as the foundation of the positive unity of all peoples, which is her chief mission. Were she not infallible, she could not guide mankind in the true way; she would be a blind leader of the blind. Finally, were she not independent, she could not fulfill her duty toward society; she would become the instrument of the powers of this world and would completely fail in her mission.

The essential and indispensable characteristics of the true Church are, it seems, settled and clear enough. Nevertheless, our modern Orthodox, after confusing the divine and the earthly aspects of the Church in their nebulous reasonings, are quite prepared to identify this muddled ideal with the present-day Eastern church, the Greco-Russian church as we see it. They affirm it to be the one and only Church of God, the true universal Church, and they regard other communions as nothing but anti-Christian associations. Thus while accepting in theory the idea of the universal Church, the Slavophils deny it in fact and reduce the worldwide character of Christianity to one particular church which in other respects is far from corresponding to the ideal which they themselves uphold. According to their notion, as we have seen, the true Church is "the organic synthesis of freedom and unity in charity," and it is in the Greco-Russian church, they say, that we are to look for this synthesis! Let us try to take them seriously and see what there is in the idea.

Chapter 5

Religious Freedom and Ecclesiastical Freedom

In the sphere of religion and of the Church, two very different things may be understood by the word *freedom*: first, the independence of the *ecclesiastical body*, both the clergy and the faithful, in relation to the external power of the state, and second, the independence of *individuals* in matters of religion, that is to say, the concession to everyone of the right to belong *openly* to such-and-such a religious body, to pass freely from one of these bodies to another, or to belong to none and to profess *with impunity* any kind of religious belief or opinion whether positive or negative.[1] To avoid confusion, we will call the former "ecclesiastical freedom" and the latter "religious freedom."[2]

Every church takes for granted a certain number of common beliefs, and anyone who does not share these beliefs cannot enjoy the same community of rights as the believers. The power to take action by spiritual means against unfaithful members and definitely to exclude them from the community is one of the essential attributes of *ecclesiastical freedom*. *Religious freedom* does not come within the particular province of the Church except indirectly; it is only the temporal power of the state which can di-

---

[1] We are not concerned here with a third kind of freedom, that of the various cults recognized by the state. A certain freedom for the cults in their status quo is imposed by the force of circumstances upon an empire such as Russia, which numbers more than thirty million subjects outside the ruling church.

[2] The expressions commonly used in the latter sense, such as "freedom of conscience" or "freedom of profession of faith," should be rejected as inexact; conscience is always free and no one can prevent a martyr from confessing his faith.

rectly admit or restrict the right of its subjects to profess openly all their individual religious beliefs. The Church can only exert a moral influence to induce the state to be more or less tolerant. No church ever regarded with indifference the propagation of strange beliefs which threatened to rob her of her faithful children.

But the question remains: What weapons should the Church employ against her enemies? Ought she to confine herself to spiritual means of persuasion, or should she have recourse to the state and avail herself of its material weapons, constraint, and persecution? The two methods of struggle against the enemies of the Church are not mutually exclusive. Those who have the necessary equipment can distinguish between intellectual error and bad faith, and, while bringing persuasion to bear on the former, can guard against the latter by depriving it of the means of doing harm.[3] But there is one essential condition if the spiritual struggle is to be even possible, namely, that the Church herself should enjoy *ecclesiastical freedom* and should not be reduced to subservience to the state. A man who has his hands tied cannot defend himself by his own efforts, but is compelled to rely on the assistance of others. A state church totally subject to the secular power and owing its continued existence to the favor of the latter has renounced its spiritual authority and can only be defended successfully by material weapons.[4]

In past times the Roman Catholic Church, which has always

---

[3] We admit this distinction in theory (in the abstract), but we are far from recommending it as a practical policy.

[4] Even our ecclesiastical writers admit as much with considerable naïveté. For instance, in a series of articles in the *Orthodox Review* (*Pravoslavnoye Obozrenie*) on the struggle of the Russian clergy against the dissenters, the author, M. Chistyakov, after exposing the exploits of Pitirim, the bishop of Nijni-Novgorod, whose zeal was invariably supported by the troops of the vice-governor Rzhevski, reaches the conclusion that the famous missionary owed all his success to the help of the secular power and to the right of bringing the dissenters by force to listen to his preaching (*Prav. Obozr.*, October 1887, 348). Similar admissions can be found in the same review (of the year 1882) with regard to contemporary missions among the pagans of Eastern Siberia.

enjoyed a measure of ecclesiastical freedom and has never been a state church, has encountered her enemies with the spiritual weapons of instruction and preaching and at the same time has authorized Catholic states to use the temporal sword in the name of religious unity. Today there are no longer any Catholic states; the state in the West is atheist, and the Roman Church continues to exist and to prosper in sole reliance upon the spiritual sword, upon her moral authority, and upon the free proclamation of her principles.

But how can a hierarchy that has committed itself to the temporal power and thereby admitted its own lack of spiritual power exert that moral authority which it has renounced? Our present established church has espoused the interests of the state to the exclusion of all else in order to receive in return the guarantee of its existence against the menace of dissent. Since the aim is a purely material one, the means are bound to be of the same character. The measures of constraint and violence prescribed by the Imperial Penal Code are in the last resort the only weapons of defense with which our "state Orthodoxy" can meet either dissent at home or religious bodies from outside which would dispute its authority over the souls of our people. If in recent times the representatives of the clergy have made certain attempts to counter the sectarians by means of semipublic discussions,[5] the lack of good faith which is only too evident in these conferences (in which one side is bound to be in the wrong whatever happens, and is able to say only what its opponents permit) has merely had the effect of revealing the moral impotence of an established church which is too accommodating to the powers that be to win respect

---

[5] I refer to the "conversations (*sobesedovanya*) with the old believers" at Kazan, at Kaluga, and especially at Moscow. Despite the irksome conditions of these discussions and the absence of the leaders of the *Raskol*, the representatives of the official church did not always have it their own way. A paper named *The Moscow Voice* (*Golos Moskvy*), which had the courage to publish in 1885 the shorthand reports of these conferences, has had reason to repent of its rashness. It no longer exists.

and too ruthless in its spiritual claims to win affection. Yet this is the church that is to exemplify for us the free union of human consciences in the spirit of charity!

The Slavophils in their anti-Catholic propaganda have labored to confuse ecclesiastical with religious freedom. Since the Catholic Church has not always been tolerant, and since she does not admit the principle of indifference in religious matters, it is only too easy to declaim against the despotism of Rome without mentioning the great prerogative of ecclesiastical freedom which Catholicism alone of all Christian communions has always maintained. But when it comes to our own case, nothing is gained by the confusion of these two freedoms since it is clear that we possess neither.

Chapter 6

Relations Between the Russian and Greek Churches. Bulgaria and Serbia

The Eastern church is not a homogeneous body. Among the various nations of which it is composed, the two most important have given it their names; its official title is the Greco-Russian church. This national dualism (which, it may be remarked in passing, is singularly reminiscent of the two feet of clay of which Archbishop Philaret speaks) suggests a concrete form in which to put the question of our ecclesiastical unity. We are concerned to discover what the real living bond is which unites the Russian and the Greek churches and makes of them a single moral organism.

We are told that the Russians and the Greeks possess a common faith and that that is the main thing. But we must inquire what is meant in this case by the word "faith" or "religion" (*vera*). True faith is that which possesses our whole soul and is seen to be the moving and guiding principle of our entire existence. The profession of one and the same abstract belief, having no influence upon conscience or life, constitutes no corporate bond and cannot truly unite anyone; it becomes a matter of indifference whether or not anyone possesses this dead faith in common with anyone else. On the other hand, unity in real faith inevitably becomes a living and active unity, a moral and practical solidarity.

If the Russian and Greek churches give no evidence of their solidarity by any vital activity, their "unity of faith" is a mere abstract formula producing no fruits and involving no obligations. A layman interested in religious questions once asked that distinguished prelate, the metropolitan Philaret,[1] what could be done to

---

[1] The reader must not be surprised to come across this name constantly in

revive the relations between the Russian church and the mother church. "But on what grounds are relations between them possible?" was the reply of the author of the Greco-Russian catechism.

Some years before this curious conversation, an incident occurred which gives us an insight into the truth of the words of the wise archbishop. William Palmer, a distinguished member of the Anglican church and of the University of Oxford, wanted to join the Orthodox church. He went to Russia and Turkey to study the contemporary situation in the Christian East and to find out on what conditions he would be admitted to the communion of the Eastern Orthodox. At St. Petersburg and at Moscow he was told that he had only to abjure the errors of Protestantism before a priest, who would thereupon administer to him the sacrament of holy chrism or confirmation. But at Constantinople he found that he must be baptized afresh. As he knew himself to be a Christian and saw no reason to suspect the validity of his baptism (which, incidentally, the Orthodox Russian church admitted without question), he considered that a second baptism would be a sacrilege. On the other hand, he could not bring himself to accept Orthodoxy according to the local rules of the Russian church, since he would then become Orthodox only in Russia while remaining a heathen in the eyes of the Greeks; and he had no wish to join a national church but to join the universal Orthodox church. No one could solve his dilemma, and so he became a Roman Catholic.

It is obvious that there are questions on which the Russian church could and ought to negotiate with the Mother See, and if these questions are carefully avoided, it is because it is a foregone conclusion that a clear formulation of them would only end in a formal schism. The jealous hatred of the Greeks for the Russians to which the latter reply with a hostility mingled with contempt —that is what governs the real relations of these two national churches in spite of their being officially in communion with one another. But even this official unity hangs upon a single hair, and

our writings; he is the only really notable character produced by the Russian church in the nineteenth century.

all the diplomacy of the clergy of St. Petersburg and Constantinople is needed to prevent the snapping of this slender thread. The will to maintain this counterfeit unity is decidedly not inspired by Christian charity, but by the dread of a fatal disclosure; for on the day on which the Russian and Greek churches formally break with one another, the whole world will see that the Ecumenical Eastern church is a mere fiction and that there exist in the East nothing but isolated national churches. That is the real motive which impels our hierarchy to adopt an attitude of caution and moderation toward the Greeks—in other words, to avoid any kind of dealings with them.[2]

As for the church of Constantinople, which in its arrogant provincialism assumes the title of "the Great Church" and "the Ecumenical Church," it would probably be glad to be rid of these northern barbarians who are only a hindrance to its Panhellenic aims. In recent times, the Patriarchate of Constantinople has been twice on the verge of anathematizing the Russian church;[3] only purely material considerations have prevented a split. The Greek church of Jerusalem, which is in fact completely subservient to that of Constantinople, depends, on the other hand, for its means of subsistence almost entirely upon Russian charity. This material dependence of the Greek clergy on Russia is of very long standing, and does in fact form the only actual basis of Greco-Russian unity. But it is clear that this purely external link is incapable of fusing the two churches into a single moral organism endowed with unity of life and action.

This conclusion will be further strengthened if we take into

---

[2] It is also the only practical reason for our still retaining the Julian calendar in defiance of the sun and the stars; no change could be made without entering into negotiations with the Greeks, which is just what our clerical circles most dread.

[3] In 1872, when the Synod of St. Petersburg refused to associate itself openly with the decisions of the Greek council which excommunicated the Bulgarians; and in 1884, when the Russian government requested the Porte to nominate two Bulgarian bishops in dioceses which the Greeks regard as entirely under their jurisdiction.

consideration the national churches of lesser importance which, being under the jurisdiction of the patriarch of Constantinople, were formerly part of the Greek church but became autocephalous as the various small states regained their political independence. The relations of these so-called churches to one another, to the metropolitan See of Byzantium, and to the Russian church are almost nonexistent. Even such purely official and conventional relations as are maintained between St. Petersburg and Constantinople are not, as far as I am aware, established between Russia and the new autocephalous churches of Rumania and Greece.

The case of Bulgaria and Serbia is worse still. It is well known that in 1872 the Greek patriarchs with the consent of the Synod of Athens excommunicated the whole Bulgarian people for reasons of national policy. The Bulgarians were condemned for their "phyletism," that is to say, their tendency to subject the church to racial and national divisions. The accusation was true; but this phyletism which was heresy among the Bulgarians was orthodoxy itself among the Greeks. The Russian church, while sympathizing with the Bulgarians, wished to rise above this political quarrel. But she could only do so by speaking in the name of the universal Church, which she had no more right to do than the Greeks. The Synod of St. Petersburg, therefore, instead of making a clear pronouncement, merely sulked at the Byzantine hierarchy and, on receiving the decisions of the council of 1872 with a request for its approval, refrained from answering one way or the other. Hence arose a state of affairs which had never been foreseen or rather had been thought impossible, according to the canons of the church. The Russian church remained in formal communion with the Greek church and in actual communion with the Bulgarian church without any explicit protest against the canonical act of excommunication which separated these two churches or any appeal, even if only for form's sake, to an ecumenical council.

A complication of the same kind arose with Serbia. The atheist government of this little kingdom promulgated ecclesiastical laws which established the hierarchy of the Serbian church on a basis of compulsory simony, since all sacred offices were to be purchased at a fixed tariff. The metropolitan, Michael, and the other bishops were arbitrarily deposed and a new hierarchy was created in defiance of canon law. This hierarchy was formally repudiated by the Russian church and replied by purchasing the support of the patriarch of Constantinople. It was now "the Great Church" which found herself in communion with two churches which were out of communion with one another.

It need hardly be added that all these national churches are simply state churches entirely without any kind of ecclesiastical freedom. It is easy to imagine the disastrous effect which such an oppression of the Church can produce upon the religion of these unfortunate countries. The religious indifference of the Serbs is as well known as their mania for using Orthodoxy as a political weapon in their fratricidal struggle against the Catholic Croats. As regards Bulgaria, Bishop Joseph, the exarch of that country and a witness of unimpeachable authority, revealed the distressing state of religion among his people in an allocution delivered at Constantinople in 1885 on the feast of St. Methodius. "The mass of the people," he said, "are cold and indifferent, while the educated classes are definitely hostile to everything sacred; it is only fear of the Russians that prevents the abolition of the church in Bulgaria."[4]

There is no need for us to show that the religious condition of Rumania and Greece is essentially the same as that of the Serbs and Bulgarians. In a report presented to the emperor of Russia by the procurator of the Holy Synod, the religious and ecclesiastical condition of the four Orthodox countries of the Balkan peninsula is painted in the darkest colors. It could not in fact be worse. But what is really surprising is the explanation given in the official document. The one and only cause of all these evils, according to the ruler of our church, is the constitutional regime! If that is so, then what is the cause of the deplorable state of the church of Russia?

---

[4] This sermon was reproduced in full in Katkov's paper, the *Moscow Gazette*.

Chapter 7

The Fulfillment of a Prophecy.
Caesaropapism in Action

George Samarin,[1] a friend of Aksakov, and like him, a prominent member of the Slavophil party or group, in a letter on the subject of the [First] Vatican Council wrote as follows:

> Papal absolutism has not killed the vitality of the Catholic clergy; this should give us food for thought, for some day or other we shall hear promulgated the infallibility of the tsar or rather that of the procurator of the Holy Synod, for the tsar is of comparatively no importance. . . . When that day comes, shall we find a single bishop, a single monk, or a single priest who will protest? I doubt it. If anyone protests it will be a layman, your obedient servant or Ivan Sergeyevich [Aksakov], if we are still in this world. As for our unfortunate clergy, whom you think deserving of pity rather than blame (and perhaps you are right), they will be dumb.

It was good fortune that brought these words to my notice, for I know few prophecies of the kind which have been fulfilled so exactly to the letter. The proclamation of caesaropapist abso-

---

[1] Yury (George) Fedorovich Samarin (d. 1876), an ardent disciple of Khomyakov, whose brilliant qualities he lacked, but whom he surpassed in learning and critical acumen, deserved well of Russia for the very active part he played in the emancipation of the serfs in 1861. Apart from that, his cultured intelligence and remarkable talent remained almost entirely unproductive, as so often happens in Russia. He left behind him no works of importance, and as a writer he chiefly distinguished himself by controversial writings against the Jesuits and the Germans of the Baltic provinces. The letter from which we quote was addressed to a Russian lady (Mme. A. O. Smirnov) and is dated December 1871.

lutism in Russia, the profound silence and absolute submission of the clergy, and finally the solitary protest of a single layman—it has all come about exactly as Samarin foresaw.

In 1885, an official document emanating from the Russian government[2] declared that the Eastern church had relinquished its authority and placed it in the hands of the tsar. Few people noticed this significant utterance. Samarin was already dead some years. Aksakov had only a few months to live; nevertheless he published in his periodical *Russ* the protest of a lay writer who incidentally did not belong to the Slavophil group. This solitary protest, neither authorized nor supported by a single representative of the church, only served by its isolation to throw into relief the deplorable state of religion in Russia.[3] Indeed, the caesaropapist manifesto of the officials of St. Petersburg was merely the explicit admission of an established fact.

It is undeniably true that the Eastern church has abdicated in favor of the secular power; the only question is whether it had the right to do so and whether, having done so, it could still represent him to whom all power has been given in heaven and on earth. Whatever violence may be done to the Gospel passages concerning the eternal powers left by Jesus Christ to his Church, they will never yield any mention of the right of surrendering those powers into the hands of a temporal authority. The authority which claims to take over the Church's mission on earth must have received at least the same promise of stability.

We do not believe that our prelates have willingly or deliberately surrendered their ecclesiastical authority. But if the Eastern

---

[2] Regulations for State Examinations in the Faculty of Laws.

[3] *Note to Russian readers*: I did not sign the article in question ("State Philosophy in the University Curricula," *Russ*, September 1885), because I believed myself to be expressing the general feelings of Russian society. This was an illusion, and I can now assert my sole claim to this *voice crying in the wilderness*. But it must not be forgotten that besides what is called "society" there are in Russia twelve to fifteen million dissenters who did not wait for the year 1885 to make their protest against the caesaropapism of Moscow and St. Petersburg.

church has in the course of events lost that which once belonged to her by divine right, it is clear that the gates of Hades have prevailed against her and that therefore she is not the impregnable Church founded by Christ.

Nor do we wish to hold the secular government responsible for the anomalous relation of the church to the state. The state has been justified in maintaining its independence and supremacy in regard to a spiritual authority which only represented one particular national church in separation from the great Christian community. The declaration that the state should be subject to the Church can only refer to the one, indivisible, and universal Church founded by God.

The government of a separated national church is only a historical and purely human institution. But the head of the state is the lawful representative of the nation as such, and a body of clergy which aims at being national and nothing more must, whether its members like it or not, recognize the absolute sovereignty of the secular government. The sphere of national existence can include within itself only one single center, the head of the state. The hierarchy of one particular church can only claim to exercise over the state the sovereignty of apostolic authority insofar as it in fact forms the link between the nation and the universal, that is, the international, kingdom of Christ. A national church that does not wish to be subject to the absolute authority of the state, that is to say, to surrender its existence as a church and become a department of the civil administration, must possess a real *point d'appui* [point of support] outside the confines of state and nation. With these it is connected by natural and historical ties; but as a church it must belong to a wider social group with an independent center and a worldwide organization of which the local church can only constitute a single, individual member.

The leaders of the Russian church could not rely on their religious metropolis in the struggle against the overpowering despotism of the state; for the Mother See was itself no more than a national church which had long been subservient to the secular power. It is not ecclesiastical freedom but caesaropapism which we

have inherited from Byzantium, where this anti-Christian principle had developed unhindered ever since the ninth century.

The Greek hierarchy, having repudiated the powerful support
which it had possessed thus far in the independent center of the
universal Church, found itself completely abandoned to the mercy
of the state and its despot. Before the schism, each time that the
Greek emperors encroached upon the spiritual domain and threatened the freedom of the Church, her spokesmen—whether it was
St. John Chrysostom, or St. Flavian, or St. Maximus the Confessor, or St. Theodore of the Studium, or the Patriarch St. Ignatius
—turned to the international center of Christendom and appealed
to the judgment of the sovereign pontiff; and if they themselves
fell victims to brute force, yet their cause, the cause of truth and
justice and freedom, never failed to find in Rome a resolute champion who ensured its ultimate triumph. In those days, the Greek
church was, and knew herself to be, a living part of the universal
Church, closely bound to the whole by the common center of
unity, the apostolic Chair of Peter. This relation of salutary dependence upon a successor of the supreme apostles, God's pontiff,
this purely spiritual, lawful, and honorable relation, gave place to
a worldly, unlawful, and humiliating subjection to the power of
mere laymen and unbelievers.

This is not simply an accident of history; it is an instance of the
logic of events which inevitably robs any merely national church
of its independence and dignity and brings it under the yoke of
the temporal power, a yoke which may be more or less oppres-
sive but is always ignominious. In every country which has been
brought to accept a national church, the secular government, be
it autocratic or constitutional, enjoys absolute authority; the ecclesiastical institution only figures as a special ministry dependent
on the general state administration. In such a case, the national
state is the real complete entity, existing by itself and for itself.
The church is only a section, or rather a certain aspect, of this
social organism of the body politic, only existing for itself in the
abstract.

Such enslavement of the Church is incompatible with its spiritual dignity, its divine origin, and its universal mission. On the other hand, reason demonstrates, and history confirms the conclusion, that it is absolutely impossible for two powers and two governments, equally sovereign and independent and confined to the same territory, to exist for long side by side within the bounds of a single national state. Such a dyarchy inevitably produces an antagonism that can only end in a complete triumph for the secular government since it is this which really represents the nation, whereas the Church by its very nature is not a national institution and cannot become one without forfeiting the true reason for its existence.

We are told that the emperor of Russia is a son of the Church. That is only what he should be as head of a Christian state. But if he is to be so in actual fact, then the Church must exercise an authority over him; she must possess a power that is independent and superior to that of the state. With the best will in the world, the secular monarch cannot be truly the son of a church of which he is at the same time the head and which he governs through his officials.

The church in Russia, deprived of any *point d'appui* or center of unity outside the national state, has inevitably come to be subservient to the secular power; and the latter, acknowledging no authority upon earth superior to itself, recognizing no one from whom it may receive religious sanction, that is to say, a partial delegation of the authority of Christ, has just as inevitably engendered an anti-Christian despotism. If the national state asserts itself as a complete and self-sufficient social organism, it cannot belong as a living member to the universal Body of Christ. And if it is outside that body, then it is not a Christian state and is only reviving the ancient Caesarism which Christianity abolished.

God assumed manhood in the person of the Jewish Messiah at the moment when a man was assuming godhead in the person of the Roman Caesar. Jesus Christ did not attack Caesar or dispute his authority; he spoke the truth about him. He said that Caesar was not God and that Caesar's power was external to the kingdom of God. The rendering to Caesar of the money that he coins and

to God of all the rest, that is what is called nowadays the separation of church and state, a separation which is essential as long
as Caesar remains pagan, but impossible as soon as he becomes
Christian.

A Christian, be he king or emperor, cannot remain outside
the kingdom of God and set up his own authority against God's.
The supreme commandment, "Render to God the things that are
God's," is necessarily binding upon Caesar himself if he would be
a Christian. He too must render to God what is God's, and to God
belongs, above all, supreme and absolute power upon earth; for
if we would understand the words about Caesar which our Lord
addressed to his enemies before his Passion, we must complete
them with that other more solemn utterance after his Resurrection. To his disciples, the representatives of his Church, he said:
"All power in heaven and on earth has been given to me" (Matt.
28:18). This is an explicit and decisive passage which cannot hon-
estly be interpreted in more than one way. Those who really believe in Christ's words will never recognize a state as an absolutely independent and sovereign temporal power, separate from
the kingdom of God. There is only one power upon earth and
that belongs not to Caesar but to Jesus Christ. The words about
the tribute-money have already robbed Caesar of his divinity; this
new utterance robs him of his despotic authority. If he wishes
to reign upon earth, he can no longer do so in his own right;
he must receive his commission from him to whom all power is
given upon earth. How, then, is he to obtain this commission?

Jesus Christ, in revealing to men the kingdom of God which is
not of this world, gave them all the necessary means of realizing
this kingdom in the world. Having affirmed in his high-priestly
prayer that the final aim of his work was the perfect unity of all,
our Lord desired to provide an actual organic basis for this work
by founding his visible Church and by giving it a single head in
the person of Peter as the guarantee of its unity. If there is in the
Gospels any delegation of authority, it is this. Jesus Christ gave
no sanction or promise whatsoever to any temporal power. He
founded only the Church, and he founded it on the monarchical

power of Peter: "You are Peter, and on this rock I will build my church" (Matt. 16:18).

The Christian state, therefore, must be dependent upon the Church founded by Christ, and the Church itself is dependent upon the head which Christ has given it. In a word, it is through Peter that the Christian Caesar must share in the kingship of Christ. He can possess no authority apart from him who has received the fullness of all authority; he cannot reign apart from him who holds the keys of the kingdom. The state, if it is to be Christian, must be subject to the Church of Christ; but if this subjection is to be genuine, the Church must be independent of the state, it must possess a center of unity outside and above the state, it must be in truth the universal Church.

It has lately begun to be realized in Russia that a merely national church, left to its own resources, is bound to become a passive and worthless instrument of the state, and that ecclesiastical independence can only be ensured by an international center of spiritual authority. But while the necessity of such a center is admitted, attempts have been made to bring it into being within the boundaries of Eastern Christendom. This plan to create an Eastern quasi-pope is the last anti-Catholic ambition left for us to examine.

Chapter 8

The Design to Establish a Quasi-Papacy at Constantinople or Jerusalem

This preconceived determination that at all costs the center of the universal Church shall be situated in the East indicates at the very outset a spirit of local egotism and racial hatred that is more likely to breed schism than to establish Christian unity. Would it not be better to put prejudice aside and look for the center of unity where it is actually to be found? If it is not to be found anywhere, it is surely childish to attempt to invent it.

Once it is granted that such a center is necessary to the normal life of the Church, it cannot be supposed that the divine head and founder of the Church did not foresee this necessity, or that he left the indispensable basis of his work to chance circumstances or human caprice. If facts compel us to admit that the Church cannot act freely without an international center of unity, we must also frankly confess that the Christian East has been deprived of this essential organ for the last thousand years and cannot therefore alone constitute the universal Church. Surely during so long a period the universal Church must have manifested her unity elsewhere.

That there is nothing serious or practical in this hybrid notion of finding a central government for the universal Church somewhere in the East or of setting up an Eastern antipope is sufficiently shown by the inability of its advocates to agree on the following question, even when put as a mere theoretical plan or a pious aspiration: On which of the dignitaries of the Eastern church is this uncertain task to devolve? Some are in favor of the "ecumenical patriarch" of Constantinople; others would prefer the See of

Jerusalem, the "Mother of all the Churches." If we here attempt briefly to do justice to these pathetic utopias, it is not because of their intrinsic importance (which is absolutely nil), but simply out of regard for certain estimable writers who in desperation have sought to substitute these imaginary notions for the true ideal of the reunion of the churches.

If the center of unity does not exist by divine right, then the Church of the present day (which they regard nevertheless as a complete organism) must create for herself, after a life of eighteen centuries, that upon which her very existence depends. It is as if a human body, all complete but for the brain, were to be expected to manufacture this central organ for itself. Since the general absurdity of the theory is not apparent to our opponents, however, we must go into their schemes in detail.

In conferring the primacy of jurisdiction upon one of her pastors, the Church may guide her choice either by the facts of religious history attested by ecclesiastical tradition or by purely political considerations. In order to lend an air of religious sanction to their national ambitions, the Greeks of Byzantium have asserted that their church was founded by the apostle Andrew to whom they give the title of *protokletos* (first-called). The legendary connection between this apostle and Constantinople, even if it were well established, could not confer any ecclesiastical prerogative on the imperial city, since neither Scripture nor the tradition of the Church attributes to Andrew any kind of primacy in the apostolic college. The apostle could hardly communicate to his church a privilege which he did not possess himself; and at the Ecumenical Council of Chalcedon in 451, the Greek bishops, desiring to attribute primacy in the East to the See of Constantinople and second place in the universal Church after the bishop of "Old Rome," carefully avoided any appeal to Andrew and based their proposal solely on the political eminence of the imperial city.

This argument, which is ultimately the only argument for the claims of Byzantium, cannot in fact justify them either in the past or in the future. If the preeminence of the "ruling city" carries with it ecclesiastical primacy, then the ancient city of Rome, which no longer enjoyed this preeminence, should have forfeited her leading place in the Church. Yet so far was anyone from daring to question her position that it was to the pope himself that the Greek bishops came with their humble request that he would deign to approve the conditional and partial primacy of the Byzantine patriarch.

As far as the situation today is concerned, what is to be done if the primacy belongs by right to that patriarch who is installed at the residence of the Orthodox emperor, seeing that there is neither Orthodox emperor at Constantinople nor patriarch at St. Petersburg? Or supposing this difficulty were overcome and Constantinople became again the ruling city of the Orthodox world and the residence of an Eastern emperor, whether Russian, Greek, or Greco-Russian—still for the Church it would be merely a return to the caesaropapism of the Eastern Empire. We know as a fact that the usurped primacy of the imperial patriarch was fatal to the freedom and authority of the Church in the East. It is clear that those who would escape the caesaropapism of St. Petersburg by removing it to Constantinople are merely jumping out of the frying pan into the fire.

Jerusalem, the hallowed center of the national theocracy of the Old Testament, has no claim to supremacy in the universal Church of Christ. Tradition calls St. James the first bishop of Jerusalem. But James had no kind of primacy in the apostolic Church any more than did Andrew, and could not therefore communicate any special privilege to his See. Besides, for a long time he had no successor.

At the approach of Vespasian's legions, the Christians deserted the condemned city which in the following century lost even its name. At the time of its restoration under Constantine, the See of James was subordinate to the jurisdiction of the metropolitan archbishop of Caesarea in Palestine, just as up to 381 the bishop of Byzantium was subordinate to the metropolitan of Heraclea in Thrace. Even after this, Jerusalem was for a long time a patriarchate in name only, and when she finally obtained independent jurisdiction, she took the last place among patriarchal sees.

Today, the "Mother of all the Churches" is reduced to a co-terie subservient to Phanariot phyletism and pursuing an exclu-sively national policy. If Jerusalem is to become the hierarchical center of the universal Church, then the Panhellenic clique must be dispossessed and a new order of things created out of nothing. But even if such an achievement were within the bounds of pos-sibility, it is obvious that Russia could only bring it about at the price of a definite rupture with the Greeks. And then what would become of the universal Church for which Russia is to provide, ready-made, an independent center of authority? A Greco-Russian church would no longer exist; and the new patriarch of Jerusalem would be in reality only the patriarch of all the Russias. Certainly the Bulgarians and Serbs would do nothing to further the inde-pendence of the Church, and so we should have come back to a national church with a hierarchy whose acknowledged leader could be no more than a mere subject and servant of the state.

The manifest impossibility of finding or creating in the East a center of unity for the universal Church makes it imperative for us to seek it elsewhere. *First and foremost, we must recognize ourselves for what we are in reality, an organic part of the great body of Christendom, and affirm our intimate solidarity with our Western brethren who possess the central organ which we lack. This moral act of justice and charity would be in itself an immense step forward on our part and the essential condition of all further advance.*

PART THREE

The Ecclesiastical Monarchy Founded by Jesus Christ

Preamble

One of the two who heard John speak, and followed him, was Andrew, Simon Peter's brother. He first found his brother Simon, and said to him, "We have found the Messiah" (which means Christ). He brought him to Jesus. Jesus looked at him, and said, "So you are Simon the son of John? You shall be called Cephas" (which means Peter) (John 1:40–42).

The Greco-Russian church, as we have seen, claims the special patronage of Andrew. The blessed apostle, inspired by goodwill toward his brother, brings him to the Lord and hears from the divine lips the first word of Simon's future destiny as the rock of the Church. There is no indication in the Gospels or in the Acts of the Apostles that Andrew ever felt any envy toward Peter or questioned his primacy. It is because we would justify the claim of Russia to be the church of Andrew that we shall try to imitate his example and to conceive the same spirit of goodwill and religious harmony toward the great Church which is especially connected with Peter. This spirit will preserve us from local or national egotism, the source of so much error, and will enable us to examine the dogma of the rock of the Church in the light of the very essence of the revelation of the God-Man, and so to discern in that revelation the eternal truths which this dogma expresses.

Chapter 1

The Rock of the Church

It would take too long to investigate here or even to enumerate all the existing doctrines and theories about the Church and its constitution. But anyone who is concerned to discover the plain truth about this fundamental problem of positive religion must be struck by the ease with which Providence has ordained that the truth may be learned. All Christians are in complete agreement on one point, namely, that Christ founded the Church; the question is how and in what terms he founded it.

Now, there is in the Gospels only one solitary text which mentions the founding of the Church in a direct, explicit, and formal manner. This fundamental text becomes clearer and clearer as the Church itself grows and develops the permanent features of its organic structure; and nowadays the opponents of the truth can generally find no other way out but that of mutilating Christ's creative word in order to adapt it to their own sectarian standpoint.[1]

> Now when Jesus came into the district of Caesarea Philippi, he asked his disciples, "Who do men say that the Son of Man is?" And they said, "Some say John the Baptist, others say Elijah, and others Jeremiah or one of the prophets." He said to them, "But who do you say that I am?" Simon Peter replied, "You are the Christ, the Son of the living God." And Jesus answered him, "Blessed are you, Simon Bar-Jona! For flesh and blood has not revealed this to you, but my Father who is in heaven. And I tell you, you are Peter, and on this rock I will build my Church, and the gates of Hades

---

[1] Thus the text in question is mutilated even in the Orthodox catechism of Archbishop Philaret of Moscow.

shall not prevail against it. I will give you the keys of the kingdom of heaven, and whatever you bind on earth shall be bound in heaven, and whatever you loose on earth shall be loosed in heaven" (Matt. 16:13–19).

The union of the divine and the human, which is the goal of creation, was accomplished individually (or hypostatically) in the unique person of Jesus Christ, "perfect God and perfect man uniting the two natures in a perfect manner without confusion and without division."[2] From this moment forward, the historic work of God enters upon a new stage. It is no longer a matter of a physical and individual unity but of a moral and social union. The God-Man desires to unite humanity with himself in a perfect union. The human race is steeped in error and sin. How shall he set about it? Is he to approach each human soul separately and unite it to himself by a purely interior and subjective bond? He answers, No: "I will build my Church." It is a real, objective work of which we are here told. But will he allow this work to be subject to all the divisions natural to the human race? Will he unite himself to individual nations as such by giving them independent national churches? No; he does not say, I will build my *churches*, but my *Church*. Mankind united to God must form a single social structure and a solid basis must be found for this unity.

Any genuine union is based on the mutual interaction of those who are united. The act of absolute truth which is revealed in the God-Man (or the perfect man) must meet with the response of imperfect humanity in an act of irrevocable adherence which links us to the divine principle. God incarnate does not desire that his truth should be accepted in a passive and servile spirit. In his new dispensation he asks of mankind a free act of recognition. But at the same time this free act must be absolutely true and infallible. Therefore, in the midst of fallen humanity, a single fixed and impregnable point must be established on which the constructive activity of God may be directly based, a point at which human freedom shall coincide with divine truth in a composite act ab-

---

[2] Formula of Pope St. Leo the Great and of the Council of Chalcedon.

solutely human in its outward form but divinely infallible in its fundamental character.

To realize the creation of the individual physical humanity of Christ, the act of the divine omnipotence required only the supremely passive and receptive self-surrender of feminine nature in the person of the Immaculate Virgin. The building up of the social or collective humanity of Christ, of his universal body, the Church, demands less and at the same time more than that: less, because the human foundation of the Church need not be represented by an absolutely pure and sinless individual, since there is no question in this case of creating a substantial and individual relation, or a hypostatic and complete union, between two natures, but simply of forging a living moral bond. If, however, this new link (the link between Christ and the Church) is less intimate and fundamental than the previous link (that between the Word of God and human nature in the womb of the Immaculate Virgin), it is humanly speaking more positive, and of more far-reaching influence: more positive, because this new bond between the Spirit and the truth demands a virile will to respond to God's revelation and a virile intelligence to give a definite form to the truth which it accepts. Moreover, this new link is of wider scope because, forming as it does the creative foundation of a collective entity, it cannot be confined to a personal relationship but must be extended through time as a permanent function of the society so formed.

It was necessary, therefore, to find in mankind as it is such a center of active coherence between the divine and the human, which might form the base or rock-foundation of the Christian Church. Jesus in his supernatural foreknowledge had already pointed out this rock. But in order to show us that his choice was free from all suspicion of arbitrariness, he begins by seeking elsewhere the human response to revealed truth. He turns first of all to general public opinion; he wishes to see whether he cannot be recognized, accepted, and acclaimed by the opinion of the mob, the voice of the people: " 'Who do men say that the Son of Man is?' " (Matt. 16:13). For whom do men take me? But truth is ever one and the same, whereas the opinions of men are many and conflicting. The voice of the people, which some claim to be the voice of God, only answered the question of the God-Man with its own erroneous and discordant opinions. No bond is possible between truth and such errors; mankind cannot enter into relation with God by the way of popular opinion; the Church of Christ cannot be founded on democracy.

Having questioned popular opinion and failed to find there man's response to divine truth, Jesus Christ turns to his chosen, the college of the apostles, that first of all ecumenical councils: " 'But who do you say that I am?' " (Matt. 16:15). But the apostles are silent. The moment before, when asked for the opinions of men, the Twelve all spoke together. Why do they leave the word to one of their number when it is a question of asserting divine truth? Possibly they are not quite agreed among themselves; possibly Philip does not perceive the essential relation of Jesus to the heavenly Father; possibly Thomas is doubtful of the messianic power of his Master. The last chapter of Matthew tells us that even on the Galilean mountain, to which Jesus summoned them after his Resurrection, the apostles did not show themselves unanimous and firm in their faith (Matt. 28:17).

If it is to bear unanimous witness to the pure and simple truth, the council must be in absolute agreement. The decisive act must be an entirely individual act, the act of a single person. It is neither the multitude of the faithful nor the apostolic council but Simon Bar-Jona alone who answers Jesus. "Simon Peter replied, 'You are the Christ, the Son of the living God' " (Matt. 16:16). He replies for all the apostles, but he speaks on his own responsibility without consulting them or waiting for their consent. When the apostles had repeated a moment before the opinions of the crowd which followed Jesus, they had only repeated what were errors; if Simon had only wished to voice the opinions of the apostles, he would possibly not have reached the pure and simple truth. But he followed his own spiritual impulse, the voice of his own conscience; and in pronouncing his solemn approval, Jesus declared that this impulse, for all its individual character, came nevertheless from his heavenly Father, that it was an act both divine and human, a real cooperation between the absolute Being and the relative subject.

The fixed point, the impregnable rock, has been discovered whereon to base the divine-human activity. The organic foundation of the universal Church is found in a single man who, with divine assistance, answers for the whole world. It is fixed neither upon the impossible unanimity of all believers nor upon the inevitably hazardous agreement of a council, but upon the real and living unity of the prince of the apostles. And from then on, every time that the question of truth is put to Christian humanity, it will not be from the voice of the masses or from the opinion of the elect that the fixed and final answer will come. The arbitrary opinions of men will only give rise to heresies; and the hierarchy separated from its center and abandoned to the mercy of the secular power will refrain from speaking or will speak through such councils as the "robber-council" of Ephesus.

Only in union with the rock on which it is founded will the Church be able to assemble true councils and define the truth by authoritative formulas. This is no mere opinion; it is a historic fact of such impressiveness that on the most solemn occasions it has been averred by the Eastern bishops themselves for all their jealousy of the successors of Peter. Not only was the wonderful dogmatic treatise of Pope St. Leo the Great recognized by the Greek fathers of the fourth ecumenical council as a work of Peter, but it was also to Peter that the sixth council attributed the letter of Pope Agatho, who was far from having the same personal authority that Leo had. "The head and prince of the apostles," declared the Eastern fathers, "fought with us. . . . The ink (of the letter) was plain to see and Peter spoke through Agatho."[3]

Otherwise, if apart from Peter the universal Church can expressly declare the truth, how are we to explain the remarkable silence of the Eastern episcopate (notwithstanding that they have kept the apostolic succession) since its separation from the Chair

---

[3] Mansi, *Sacrorum Conciliorum*, 11:658.

of Peter? Can it be merely an accident? An accident lasting for a thousand years! To those anti-Catholics who will not see that their particularism cuts them off from the life of the universal Church, we have only one suggestion to make: Let them summon, without the concurrence of the successor of Peter, a council which they themselves can recognize as ecumenical! Then only will there be an opportunity of discovering whether or not they are right.

Wherever Peter does not speak, only the opinions of men find utterance—and the apostles are silent. But Jesus Christ did not commend the vague and contradictory opinions of the mob or the silence of his chosen disciples; it was the unwavering, decisive, and authoritative utterance of Simon Bar-Jona upon which he set the seal of his approval. This utterance which satisfied our Lord clearly needed no human ratification; it possessed absolute validity *etiam sine consensu Ecclesiae.*[4] It was not by means of a general consultation but (as Jesus Christ himself bore witness) with the direct assistance of the heavenly Father that Peter formulated the fundamental dogma of our religion; and his word defined the faith of Christians by its own inherent power, not by the consent of others—*ex sese, non autem ex consensu Ecclesiae.*[5]

In contrast to the uncertain opinions of men, the word of Peter represents the stability and unity of the true faith; in contrast to the narrow national ideas of the Messiah to which the apostles gave utterance, his word expresses the messianic idea in its absolute and universal form. The idea of the Messiah which had sprung from the soil of Jewish national consciousness is already in the visions of the post-exilic prophets growing too large for these limits. But the true meaning of these mysterious and enigmatic visions was hardly divined by the inspired writers themselves, while Jewish public opinion remained exclusively nationalistic and could see no more in Christ than a great national prophet such as Elijah, Jeremiah, or John the Baptist, or at the most an all-powerful dic-

---

[4] "Even without the consent of the Church," the formula of the First Vatican Council.

[5] "Of itself, and not by the consent of the Church."—ED.

tator, liberator, and leader of the chosen people such as Moses or David. This was the highest idea that the mob which followed Jesus held of him; and we know that even his chosen disciples shared these popular notions up to the end of his earthly life (cf. Luke 24:19–21).

Only in Peter's confession does the messianic idea emerge, freed from all its nationalistic trappings and invested for the first time in its final and universal form. "You are the Christ, the Son of the living God" (Matt. 16:16). Here is no question of a national king or prophet; the Messiah is not a second Moses or David. From this time on, he bears the unique name of him who, though he is the God of Israel, is nonetheless the God of all the nations. Peter's confession transcended Jewish nationalism and inaugurated the universal Church of the New Covenant.

This is yet one more reason why Peter should be the foundation of Christendom and why the supreme hierarchical authority, which of itself has ever maintained the universal or international character of the Church, should be the true heir of Peter and the actual possessor of all those privileges conferred by Christ upon the prince of the apostles.

Chapter 2

The Primacy of Peter as a Permanent Institution.
The Three Rocks of Christendom

"And I tell you, you are Peter . . ." (Matt. 16:18). Of the three attributes represented in this crucial passage as belonging by divine right to the prince of the apostles—1) the call to be the foundation of the Church by the infallible confession of the truth, 2) the possession of the power of the keys, 3) the power of binding and loosing—it is only the last that he shares with the other apostles.

All Orthodox Christians[1] are agreed that the apostolic power of binding and loosing was not conferred upon the Twelve as private individuals or in the sense of a temporary privilege, but that it is the genuine source and origin of a perpetual priestly authority which has descended from the apostles to their successors in the hierarchy, the bishops and priests of the *universal* Church. But if this is true, then neither can the two former attributes connected particularly with Peter in a still more solemn and significant manner be individual or accidental prerogatives;[2] the less so, in that it was with the first of these prerogatives that our Lord expressly connected the permanence and stability of his Church in its future struggle against the powers of evil.

If the power of binding and loosing conferred on the apostles

---

[1] And, among non-Orthodox, all writers who are in good faith; for instance, the eminent Jewish thinker Joseph Salvador in his book *Jesus Christ and His Work*.

[2] The notable Jewish writer already referred to accepts this conclusion wholeheartedly. He sees in the primacy of Peter the keystone of the edifice of the Church as designed and founded by Christ himself.

is not a mere metaphor or a purely personal and temporary attribute, if it is, on the contrary, the actual living seed of a universal, permanent institution comprising the Church's whole existence, how can Peter's own special prerogatives, announced in
such explicit and solemn terms, be regarded as barren metaphors
or as personal and transitory privileges? Ought not they also to refer to some fundamental and permanent institution, of which the
historic personality of Simon Bar-Jona is but the outstanding and
typical representative? The God-Man did not establish ephemeral
institutions. In his chosen disciples he saw, through and beyond all
that was mortal and individual, the enduring principles and types
of his work. What he said to the college of the apostles included
the whole priestly order, the teaching Church in its entirety.

The sublime words which he addressed to Peter alone created
in the person of this one apostle the undivided, sovereign authority possessed by the universal Church throughout the whole of
its life and development in future ages. That Christ did not see fit
to make the formal foundation of his Church and the guarantee
of its permanence dependent on the common authority of all the
apostles (for he did not say to the apostolic college: "On you I
will build my church") surely shows that our Lord did not regard
the episcopal and priestly order, represented by the apostles in
common, as sufficient in itself to form the impregnable foundation of the universal Church, in her inevitable struggle against the
gates of Hades. In founding his visible Church, Jesus was thinking
primarily of the struggle against evil; and in order to ensure for
his creation that unity which is strength, he crowned the hierarchy with a single, central institution, absolutely indivisible and
independent, possessing in its own right the fullness of authority
and of promise: "You are Peter, and on this rock I will build my
church, and the gates of Hades shall not prevail against it" (Matt.
16:18).

All arguments in support of the supreme central authority of
the universal Church would in our view have but little weight
if they were only arguments. But they rest upon a divine-human
fact which remains essential to the Christian faith despite all the

artificial interpretations by which men have attempted to suppress it. It is not for us to demonstrate the abstract necessity of an institution to which Christ has given a living actuality. The arguments of Eastern theologians demonstrating that the whole hierarchical system is essential to the Church would not suffice to convince us, were it not for the original fact recorded in the Gospels, namely, the choice of the twelve apostles to teach all nations to the end of time. Similarly, when we wish to prove that an indivisible center is essential to this same hierarchy, it is the fact of the special choice of Peter to serve as a human *point d'appui* for the divine truth in its constant struggle against the gates of Hades—it is the fact of this unique choice which provides a firm foundation for all our arguments.

If "the Church" is taken to mean the perfect union of mankind with God, the absolute reign of love and truth, then there is no place in the Church for any power or authority. All the members of this heavenly kingdom are priests and kings and, as such, are equal with one another, and the one and only center of unity is Jesus Christ himself. But it is not in this sense that we speak of the Church, for it is not in this sense that Christ spoke of it. The perfect Church, the Church triumphant, the kingdom of glory— all this implies that the power of evil and the gates of Hades are finally vanquished, and yet it is to contend with the gates of Hades that Christ builds his visible Church and gives it a center of unity which is human and earthly, though always divinely assisted.

If we would avoid the two opposite pitfalls of blind materialism and ineffectual idealism, we must admit that the needs of actual existence and the demands of the ideal coincide and harmonize in the order established by God. So as to show forth in the Church the ideal of harmony among men, Jesus Christ founded—as the prototype of conciliar government—the college or original council of the twelve apostles, equal with one another and united by brotherly love. In order that this ideal unity might be effectually realized in every age and place, that the council of the hierarchy might always and everywhere prevail over discord and gather up the multiplicity of private opinions into uniform public decrees, that discussion might issue in the living manifestation of the unity of the Church, secure from the hazards to which the assemblies of men are exposed—in a word, that his Church might not be built upon shifting sands—the divine architect revealed the firm, impregnable rock of ecclesiastical monarchy and set up the ideal of unanimity while basing it upon an actual living authority.

Christ, we are told, is the rock of the Church. That is true; no Christian has ever disputed it. But it is hard to see the reasonableness, even if we admit the sincerity, of those who, in their zeal to defend Christ from an imaginary insult, persist in ignoring his express will and in repudiating the order which he established in so explicit a manner. For he not only declared that Simon, one of his apostles, was the rock of his Church, but in order to impress this new truth more forcibly upon us and to make it more evident and striking, he gave to Simon a distinctive and permanent name derived from this very call to be the rock of the Church.

We have here, then, two equally indisputable truths: Christ is the rock of the Church, and Simon Bar-Jona is the rock of the Church. But the contradiction, if there is one, does not stop here. For we find this very Simon Peter, even though he alone received from Christ this unique prerogative, declaring in one of his epistles that all the faithful are living stones in the divine-human building (1 Pet. 2:4, 5). Jesus is the one and only rock of the Church; but, if we are to believe Jesus, the prince of the apostles is the rock of his Church par excellence; and again, if we would believe Peter, every true believer is the rock of the Church.

Confronted with the apparent inconsistency of these truths, it is enough for us to observe their actual agreement in logic. Jesus Christ, the unique rock of the kingdom of God on the purely religious and mystical plane, sets up the prince of the apostles and his permanent authority as the fundamental rock of the Church in the social order for the Christian community; and each member of this community, united to Christ and abiding in the order he established, becomes an organic individual element, a living stone of this Church whose mystical and (for the time being) invisible foundation is Jesus Christ, and whose social and visible foundation is the monarchical power of Peter. The essential distinction among these three factors only serves to throw into stronger relief the intimate connection among them in the Church's actual existence, in which Christ, Peter, and the multitude of the faithful each play an essential part.

The notion of such a threefold relationship can appear inconsistent only to those who presuppose such inconsistency by interpreting the three fundamental factors in an absolute and exclusive sense which is entirely inappropriate to them. What they forget is that the expression "rock (i.e., foundation) of the Church" is a relative expression, and that Christ can only be the rock of the Church in that definite union of himself with mankind which forms the Church; and since this union is primarily brought about in the social order through a central point of contact which Christ himself associated with Peter, it is obvious that these two Rocks —the Messiah and his chief apostle—so far from being mutually exclusive, are simply two inseparable factors in a unique relationship. As regards the rock or stones of the third order—the multitude of the faithful—though it is said that each believer may become a living stone of the Church, it is not said that he may do so by himself or in separation from Christ and the fundamental authority that he set up.

The foundation of the Church, speaking in general terms, is the union of the divine and the human. This foundation (the rock) we find in Jesus Christ inasmuch as he unites the Godhead hypostatically with sinless human nature; we find it also in every true Christian inasmuch as he is united to Christ by the sacraments, by faith, and by good works. But is it not clear that these two modes of union between the divine and the human (the hypostatic union in the person of Christ, and the individual union of the believer with Christ) are not in themselves sufficient to constitute the specific unity of the Church in the strict sense of the word—that is, as a social and historic entity? The Incarnation of the Word is a mystical fact and not a social principle; nor does the individual religious life provide an adequate basis for Christian society: man may remain alone in the desert and live a life of holiness. And yet if, besides the mystical life and the individual life, the social life exists in the Church, this social life must have a definite form based upon a unifying principle peculiar to itself.

When we maintain that this specific principle of social unity in the Church is in the first place neither Jesus Christ nor the mass of the faithful but the monarchical authority of Peter, by means of which Jesus Christ has willed to unite himself to man as a social and political being, we find our opinion confirmed by the remarkable fact that only in the case of the prince of the apostles has the attribute of being the rock of the Church carried with it the title to a distinctive and permanent name. He alone is the rock of the Church in the special and strict sense of the term, that is to say, the unifying basis of the historic Christian society.

Three times only in the whole of sacred history recorded in the two testaments did the Lord himself change a man's name. When Abram, by an act of unlimited faith vowed himself to the living God, God changed his name to Abraham ("father of the multitude") and pronounced him to be the father of all believers. When Jacob in that mysterious struggle pitted the whole spiritual energy of man against the living God, God gave him a new name ("Israel," "he who strives with God") and marked him out as the direct parent of that peculiar and unique race which has striven and still strives with its God. When Simon Bar-Jona, the descendant of Abraham and Jacob, combined in himself the powerful initiative of the human soul and the infallible assistance of the heavenly Father in the affirmation of the divine-human truth, the God-Man changed his name ("Peter," "rock") and set him at the head of the new believers and the new Israel.

Abraham, the type of primitive theocracy, represents humanity in devotion and self-surrender to God; Israel, the type of the national theocracy of the Jews, represents humanity beginning its struggle with God; and, lastly, Simon Peter, the type of universal and final theocracy, represents humanity making its response to its God, freely avowing him and cleaving to him in mutual and indissoluble adherence. That boundless faith in God which made Abraham the father of all believers was in Peter united to that active assertion of the power of man which distinguished Jacob-Israel; the prince of the apostles reflected in the earthly mirror of his soul that harmony between the divine and the human which he saw brought to perfection in his Master; and he became thereby the firstborn and principal heir of the God-Man, the spiritual father of the new Christian race, the foundation-stone of that universal Church which is the fulfillment and perfection of the religion of Abraham and of the theocracy of Israel.

Chapter 3

"Peter" and "Satan"

It was not Simon's apostleship that involved his change of name, for the change, though already predicted, was not made at the time of the choice and solemn sending forth of the Twelve. All with the single exception of Simon retained their own names in the apostleship; none of them received from our Lord a new and permanent title of wider or higher significance.[1]

Apart from Simon, all the apostles are distinguished from one another solely by their natural characteristics, their individual qualities and destinies, as well as by the varieties and shades of personal feeling shown toward them by their Master. On the other hand, the new and significant name which Simon alone receives in addition to the apostleship shared by all, indicates no natural trait in his character, no personal affection felt for him by our Lord, but refers solely to the special place which the son of Jona is called to fill in the Church of Christ. Our Lord did not say to him: You are Peter because I prefer you to the others, or because by nature you have a firm and stable character (which, incidentally, would hardly have been borne out by the facts), but: "You are Peter, and on this rock I will build my church" (Matt. 16:18).

Peter's confession, which by a spontaneous and infallible act of allegiance established the bond between mankind and Christ and founded the free Church of the New Covenant, was not just a piece of characteristic behavior on his part. Nor can it have been a casual and momentary spiritual impulse. For is it conceivable that

---

[1] I am not speaking of surnames or of casual, incidental epithets such as that of Boanerges [Sons of Thunder] given to John and James.

such an impulse or moment of enthusiasm should involve not merely a change of name for Simon as for Abraham and Jacob in times past, but also the prediction of that change long beforehand as something which would infallibly come about and which held a prominent place in our Lord's plans? Was there in fact any part of the work of the Messiah more solemn than the foundation of the universal Church which is expressly connected with Simon under his new name of Peter? Moreover, the notion that the first dogmatic decree of Peter came from him merely in his capacity as an individual human being is totally excluded by the direct and explicit witness of Christ: "Flesh and blood has not revealed this to you, but my Father who is in heaven" (Matt. 16:17).

This confession of Peter is, then, an act *sui generis*, an act whereby the moral being of the apostle entered into a special relationship with the Godhead; it was this relationship which enabled human utterance to declare infallibly the absolute truth of the Word of God and to create an impregnable foundation for the universal Church. And as though to remove all possible doubt on the subject, the inspired record of the Gospel at once goes on to show us this very Simon, whom Jesus has just declared to be the rock of the Church and the key-bearer of the kingdom of heaven, immediately left to his own resources and speaking—with the best intentions in the world, no doubt, but without divine assistance —under the influence of his own individual and uninspired personality:

> From that time Jesus began to show his disciples that he must go to Jerusalem and suffer many things from the elders and chief priests and scribes, and be killed, and on the third day be raised. And Peter took him and began to rebuke him, saying, "God forbid, Lord! This shall never happen to you." But he turned and said to Peter, "Get behind me, Satan! You are a hindrance to me; for you are not on the side of God, but of men" (Matt. 16:21-23).

Are we to follow our Greco-Russian controversialists in placing this text in opposition to the one before it and so make Christ's words cancel one another out? Are we to believe that the incarnate truth changed his mind so quickly and revoked in a moment what he had only just announced? And yet on the other hand how are we to reconcile "blessed" and "Satan"? How is it conceivable that he who is for our Lord himself a "rock of hindrance" should yet be the rock of his Church which the gates of Hades cannot shake? Or that one who thinks only the thoughts of men can receive the revelation of the heavenly Father and can hold the keys of the kingdom of God?

There is only one way to harmonize these passages which the inspired evangelist has with good reason placed side by side. Simon Peter as supreme pastor and doctor of the universal Church, assisted by God and speaking in the name of all, is the faithful witness and infallible exponent of divine-human truth; as such, he is the impregnable foundation of the house of God and the key-bearer of the kingdom of Heaven. The same Simon Peter as a private individual, speaking and acting by his natural powers and merely human intelligence, may say and do things that are unworthy, scandalous, and even diabolical. But the failures and sins of the individual are ephemeral, while the social function of the ecclesiastical monarch is permanent. "Satan" and the "hindrance" have vanished, but Peter has remained.

Chapter 4

The Church as a Universal Society.
The Principle of Love

Since the existence of every human society is determined by its ideals and institutions, it follows that social progress and well-being depend primarily on the truth of the predominant ideals of the society and on the good order which prevails in its administration. The Church as a society directly willed and founded by God must possess these two qualities to an outstanding degree: the religious ideals which she professes must be infallibly true; and her constitution must combine the greatest stability with the greatest capacity for action in any direction desired.

The Church is above all a society founded on truth. The basic truth of the Church is the union of the divine and the human in the Word made flesh, the recognition of the Son of Man as the Christ, the Son of the living God. In its purely objective aspect, therefore, the rock of the Church is Christ himself, truth incarnate. But if she is to be actually founded on the truth, the Church as a human society must be united to this truth in a definite manner.

Since, in this world of appearances, truth has no existence which is directly manifest or externally necessary, man can only establish contact with it through faith which links him to the interior substance of things and presents to his intelligence all that is not externally visible. From the subjective point of view, then, it may be asserted that it is faith which constitutes the basis or "rock" of the Church. But what faith, and on whose part? The mere fact of a subjective faith on the part of such-and-such a person is not sufficient. Individual faith of the strongest and most sincere kind may put us in touch not only with the invisible substance of truth and the sovereign good, but also with the invisible substance of evil and falsehood, as is abundantly proved by the history of religion. If man is truly to be linked by faith to the desirable object of faith, namely, absolute truth, he must be conformed to this truth.

The truth of the God-Man, that is to say, the perfect and living union of the absolute and the relative, of the infinite and the finite, of the Creator and the creature—this supreme truth cannot be limited to a historic fact, but reveals through that fact a universal principle which contains all the riches of wisdom and embraces all in its unity.

Since the objective truth of faith is universal and the true subject of faith must be conformed to its object, it follows that the subject of true religion is necessarily universal. Real faith cannot belong to man as an isolated individual but only to mankind as a complete unity; and the individual can only share in it as a living member of the universal body. But since no real and living unity has been bestowed on the human race in the physical order, it must be created in the moral order. The limits of natural egoism, of finite individuality with its exclusive self-assertion, must be burst by love which renders man conformable to God who is love. But this love which is to transform the discordant fragments of the human race into a real and living unity, the universal Church, cannot be a mere vague, subjective, and ineffectual sentiment; it must be translated into a consistent and definite activity which will give the inner sentiment its objective reality.

What, then, is the actual object of this active love? Natural love, which has for its object those beings who are nearest to us, creates a real collective unity, the family; the wider natural love which has for its object all the people of one country or one tongue creates a more extensive and more complex, but equally real, collective unity, the city, state, or nation.[1] The love which is to create the

---

[1] The fact of dwelling in the same country or speaking a common language is not sufficient in itself to produce the unity of the fatherland; that is impossible without patriotism, that is to say, without a specific love.

religious unity of the human race, or the universal Church, must surpass the bounds of nationality and have for its object the sum total of mankind. But since the active relationship between the sum total of the human race and the individual finds no basis in the latter in any natural sentiment analogous to that which animates the family or the fatherland, it is (for the individual subject) inevitably reduced to the purely moral essence of love, that is, to the free and conscious surrender of the will and the individual egoism of family or nation.

Love for one's family or for one's country is primarily a natural fact which may secondarily produce moral acts; love for the Church is essentially a moral act, the act of submitting the particular will to the universal will. But the universal will, if it is to be anything more than a fiction, must be continually realized in a definite being. The will of all humanity is not a real unity, since all men are not in direct agreement with one another; some means of harmonizing them must therefore be found, that is to say, one single will capable of unifying all the others. Each individual must be able to unite himself effectively with the whole of the human race (and thus give positive witness to his love for the Church) by linking his will to a unique will, no less real and living than his own, but at the same time a will which is universal and to which all other wills must be equally subject. But a will is inconceivable apart from one who wills and expresses his will; and inasmuch as all are not directly one, we have no choice but to unite ourselves to all in the person of one individual if we would share in the true universal faith.

Since each individual man cannot be the proper subject of universal faith any more than can the whole of mankind in its natural state of division, it follows that this faith must be manifested in a single individual, representative of the unity of all. Each individual, by taking this truly universal faith as the criterion of his own faith, makes a real act of submission to, or love for, the Church, an act which makes him conformable to the universal truth revealed to the Church. In loving all in one individual (since it is impossible to love them otherwise), each one shares in the faith of all, defined by the divinely assisted faith of a single individual; and this enduring bond, this unity so wide and yet so stable, so living and yet so unchanging, makes the universal Church a collective moral entity, a true society far more extensive and more complex but no less real than nation or state.

Love for the Church is manifested in a constant adherence to her will and her living thought represented by the public acts of the supreme ecclesiastical authority. This love, which is originally nothing but an act of pure morality, the fulfillment of a duty on principle (obedience to the categorical imperative, according to the Kantian terminology), can and must become the source of sentiments and affections no less strong than filial love or patri- otism. Those who agree with us in founding the Church upon love and yet see worldwide ecclesiastical unity only in a fossilized tradition which for eleven centuries has lost all means of actual self-expression, should bear in mind that it is impossible to love with a living and active love what is simply an archaeological relic, a remote fact, such as the seven ecumenical councils, which is ab- solutely unknown to the masses and can only appeal to the learned. Love for the Church has no real meaning except for those who recognize perpetually in the Church a living representative and a common father of all the faithful, capable of being loved as a father is loved in his family or the head of the state in a kingdom.

It is of the nature of truth to draw into a harmonious unity the manifold elements of reality. This formal characteristic belongs to the supreme truth, the truth of the God-Man, which embraces in its absolute unity all the fullness of divine and human life. The Church, which is a collective being aspiring to perfect unity, must correspond to Christ, the one being and center of all beings. And inasmuch as this interior and perfect unity of all is not realized, inasmuch as the faith of each individual is not yet in itself the faith of all, inasmuch as the unity of all is not directly manifested by each, it must be brought about by means of a single individual.

The universal truth, perfectly realized in the single person of Christ, draws to itself the faith of all, infallibly defined by the voice of a single individual, the pope. Outside this unity, as we have seen, the opinion of the masses may be mistaken and the faith even of the elect may remain in suspense. But it is neither false opinion nor a vacillating faith, but a definite and infallible faith which unites mankind to the divine truth and forms the impregnable foundation of the universal Church. This foundation is the faith of Peter living in his successors, a faith which is personal, that it may be manifest to men, and which is (by divine assistance) superhuman, that it may be infallible.

We shall not cease to challenge those who deny the necessity of such a permanent center of unity to point to any living unity in the universal Church apart from it, to produce apart from it a single ecclesiastical act which concerns the whole of Christendom, or to give, without appealing to it, a decisive and authoritative reply to a single one of the questions which divide the consciences of Christians. It is of course obvious that the present successors of the apostles at Constantinople or at St. Petersburg are imitating the silence of the apostles themselves at Caesarea Philippi.

To summarize briefly the foregoing reflections: The universal Church is founded on truth affirmed by faith. Truth being one, true faith must be one also. And since this unity of faith has no present and immediate existence among the whole mass of believers (for in religious matters all are not unanimous), it must reside in the lawful authority of a single head, guaranteed by divine assistance and accepted by the love and confidence of all the faithful. That is the rock on which Christ has founded his Church, and the gates of Hades shall not prevail against it.

Chapter 5

The Keys of the Kingdom

It seems as if Jesus wished to leave no possible doubt as to the intent and bearing of his words regarding the rock of the Church. He therefore completed them by explicitly committing the power of the keys and the supreme government of his kingdom to that fundamental authority of the Church which he established in the person of Simon Peter. "I will give you the keys of the kingdom of heaven" (Matt. 16:19).

And here we must first of all clear up a contradiction which our "Orthodox" controversialists ascribe to Jesus Christ. In order to eliminate as far as possible the distinction between Peter and the other apostles, it is asserted that the power of the keys is nothing else but the power of binding and loosing; after saying, "I will give you the keys," Jesus is supposed to have repeated the same promise in other words. But in speaking of keys, the words *shut* and *open* should have been used, not *bind* and *loose*, as in fact (to confine ourselves solely to the New Testament) we read in Revelation: "[He] who has the key of David, who opens and no one shall shut, who shuts and no one opens" (Rev. 3:7). A room, a house, or a city may be shut and opened, but only particular beings or objects situated within the room or house or city can be bound and unbound. The Gospel passage in question is a metaphor, but a metaphor is not necessarily an absurdity. The symbol of the keys of the kingdom (of the royal dwelling— *beth-ha-melek*) must necessarily represent a wider and more general authority than the symbol of binding and loosing.

The special power of binding and loosing having been bestowed upon Peter in the same terms as those in which it was conferred later on the other apostles (Matt. 18:18), it is plain from the context of the latter chapter that this lesser power only concerns in-dividual cases ("If your brother sins against you" [Matt. 18:15], etc.), which is in entire agreement with the sense of the metaphor used in the Gospel. Only personal problems of conscience and the direction of individual souls fall under the authority to bind and loose which was given to the other apostles after Peter, whereas the power of the keys of the kingdom conferred solely on Peter can only refer to the whole of the Church (if we are to follow not only the exact sense of our text, but general biblical analogy) and must denote a supreme social and political authority: the general administration of the kingdom of God on earth. The life of the Christian soul must neither be separated from the organization of the universal Church nor be confused with it. They are two different orders of things though closely interconnected.

Just as the teaching of the Church is no mere compound of per-sonal beliefs, so the government of the Church cannot be reduced to the direction of individual consciences or of private morality. Founded on unity of faith, the universal Church as a real and living social organism must also display unity of action sufficient to react successfully at every moment of her historic existence against the combined attacks of those hostile forces which would divide and destroy her. Unity of action for a vast and complicated social organism implies a whole system of organic functions sub-ordinate to a common center which can set them in motion in the direction desired at any given moment. As the unity of the orthodox faith is finally guaranteed by the dogmatic authority of a single individual speaking for all, so unity of ecclesiastical action is necessarily conditioned by the directing authority of a single individual bearing sway over the whole Church. But in the one holy Church, founded upon truth, government cannot be sepa-rated from doctrine; and the central and supreme power in the ec-clesiastical sphere can only belong to him who, by divinely aided authority, represents and displays in the religious sphere the unity of true faith.

This is why the keys of the kingdom have been given to none other than him who is by his faith the rock of the Church.

Chapter 6

The Government of the Universal Church. The Center of Unity

The Church is not only the perfect union of mankind with God in Christ, but it is also the social order established by the divine will in which and through which this union of the divine and the human may be accomplished. Founded on eternal truth, the Church is not only the perfect life (in the future), but it has also always been in the past, and still is in the present, the way which leads to this ideal perfection. Man's social existence upon earth cannot be excluded from the new union of the human and the divine which is accomplished in Christ.

If the elements even of our material life are transformed and sanctified in the sacraments, how can the social and political order, which is an essential form of human existence, be left prey to the warfare of selfish ambitions, the clash of murderous passions, and the conflict of erroneous opinions? Since man is essentially a social being, the ultimate aim of the working of God in mankind is the creation of a perfect universal society. But it is not a creation out of nothing; for the material of the perfect society is given us, namely, society in its imperfect state, mankind as it is; and this is neither excluded nor suppressed by the kingdom of God, but is drawn into the sphere of the kingdom, to be regenerated, sanctified, and transfigured.

The religion which seeks to bind man's individual being to Christ is not content with an invisible and purely spiritual communion; it desires that man should communicate with his God throughout his entire being, even by the physical act of feeding. In this mystical but real Communion the matter of the sacrament is not simply destroyed and annihilated, it is transubstantiated, that is to say, the interior and invisible substance of the bread and wine is lifted into the sphere of Christ's ascended bodily nature and absorbed by it, while the phenomenal reality or outward appearance of these objects remains without sensible change, that they may act in the given conditions of our physical existence and so establish a link between that existence and the body of God. So also must the collective, common life of mankind be mystically transubstantiated while retaining the "species" or outward forms of earthly society, and these very forms must be duly ordained and consecrated to serve as the actual foundation and visible instruments of the social activity of Christ in his Church.

The ultimate aim of the work of God in mankind, regarded from the Christian standpoint, is not the manifestation of the divine power—that is the Muslim conception—but the free, mutual union of mankind with God. And the proper means of accomplishing this work is not the hidden operation of Providence guiding individuals and nations by unknown ways to uncomprehended ends; such a purely and exclusively supernatural operation, though always necessary, is not sufficient in itself. Moreover, since the actual historic union of God and man in Christ, man must himself play a positive part in his appointed destiny and, as a social being, communicate in the life of Christ. But if mortal men here below are actually to have a real share in the invisible and supernatural government of Christ, then that government must assume visible and natural social forms. Some kind of social institution, whose origin, end, and powers are divine, while its means of action are human and adapted to the needs of historic existence, is essential to represent and minister to the perfection of divine grace and truth in Jesus Christ, that this perfection may operate in, and cooperate with, imperfect human nature.

If the Church is to guide the common life of mankind toward the goal of divine love, and to direct public opinion on the road to divine truth, she must possess a universal government divinely authorized. This government must be clearly defined, so as to be recognizable to all, and permanent, so as to form a standing court

of appeal; it must be divine in substance, so as to be finally binding upon the religious conscience of every instructed and well-
intentioned person, and it must be human and imperfect in its
historic manifestation, so as to admit the possibility of moral resistance and allow room for doubts, struggle, temptations, and all
that constitutes the merit of free and genuinely human virtue.

The supreme authority of the Church may admit of various
administrative forms according to differences of time and place,
yet if it is to form the primary basis of union between the social
conscience of mankind and the providential government of God,
and to share in the divine majesty while adapting itself to the real-
ities of human life, it must always, as the center of unity, preserve
its purely monarchical character. If the supreme authority of the
universal Church were vested solely in the collective administration of a council, the unity of her human activity linking her to
the absolute unity of divine truth could only be based on one of
two things: either on the perfect unanimity of all its members, or
else on a majority of opinions, as in secular assemblies.

The latter supposition is incompatible with the majesty of God,
who would be obliged constantly to accommodate his will and
his truth to the chance convergences of human opinion and the
interplay of human passions. As for unanimity or complete and
permanent harmony, such a condition of the social conscience
could, by its intrinsic moral excellence, undoubtedly correspond
to the divine perfection and infallibly manifest the action of God
in mankind. But while the political principle of a majority vote
comes short of the dignity of God, the ideal principle of immediate, spontaneous, and permanent unanimity is, unfortunately,
equally far in advance of the present state of man. That perfect
unity which Jesus Christ in his high-priestly prayer held up before us as the final objective of his work cannot be assumed as
the present and obvious starting point of that work. The surest
way never to achieve the desired perfection is to imagine that it
is already achieved.

Conscious unanimity and solidarity, brotherly love and free
agreement, such is the universally accepted ideal of the Church.

But the difference between an idle dream and the divine ideal of unity is that the latter has an actual foundation from which to gain ground little by little on earth and to achieve gradual and successive conquests over all the powers of discord. A real and indivisible principle of unity is absolutely necessary to counteract the deep-seated and active tendency toward division in the world and even in the Church itself. The principle of that universal religious unity of grace and truth, which is eventually to become the very essence of the life of each individual believer and the perfect and indissoluble bond between him and his neighbor, must nonetheless in the meantime have an objective existence and act everywhere under the "species" of a visible and definite social authority.

The perfection of the one universal Church consists in the harmony and unanimity of all its members; but its very existence amid actual disharmony requires a unifying and reconciling power immune from this disharmony and in continual reaction against it, asserting itself above all divisions and gathering to itself all men of goodwill, denouncing and condemning whatever is opposed to the kingdom of God on earth. Whoever desires that kingdom must desire the only way that will lead mankind collectively to it. Between the hateful reality of the disharmony reigning in this world and the longed-for unity of perfect love in which God reigns is the necessary road of a juridical and authoritative unity linking human fact to divine right.

The perfect circle of the universal Church requires a unique center, not so much for its perfection as for its very existence. The Church upon earth, called to gather in the multitude of the nations, must, if she is to remain an active society, possess a definite universal authority to set against national divisions; if she is to enter the current of history and undergo continual change and adaptation in her external circumstances and relationships and yet preserve her identity, she requires an authority essentially conservative but nevertheless active, fundamentally unchangeable though outwardly adaptable; and, finally, if she is set amid the frailty of man to assert herself in reaction against all the powers of evil, she must be equipped with an absolutely firm and impregnable foundation, stronger than the gates of Hades.

Now, we know on the one hand that Christ foresaw the necessity of such an ecclesiastical monarchy and therefore conferred supreme and undivided authority over his Church on a single individual; and on the other hand we see that, of all the ecclesiastical powers in the Christian world, only one perpetually and unchangingly preserves its central and universal character and at the same time is specially connected by an ancient and widespread tradition with him to whom Christ said: "You are Peter, and on this rock I will build my church, and the gates of Hades shall not prevail against it" (Matt. 16:18). Christ's words could not remain without their effect in Christian history; and the principal phenomenon in Christian history must have an adequate cause in the word of God. Where, then, have Christ's words to Peter produced a corresponding effect except in the Chair of Peter? Where does that chair find an adequate cause except in the promise made to Peter?

The living truths of religion do not compel the reason in the manner of geometrical theorems. Moreover, it would be unsafe to assert that everyone unanimously accepts even the truths of mathematics for the sole reason of their intrinsic proof; they meet with general acceptance because no one is concerned to reject them. I am not so simple as to hope to convince those who are influenced by other motives more powerful than the search for religious truth. In setting out the general proofs of the permanent primacy of Peter as the foundation of the universal Church, my only aim has been to assist the intellectual task of those who deny this truth not from personal or emotional reasons, but from unconscious error and inherited prejudice. In pursuance of this aim, I must now, while keeping my eyes always fixed on the brilliant searchlight of the biblical record, embark for a moment on the dark and uncertain domain of universal history.

Chapter 7

The Monarchies Foretold by Daniel.
"Roma" and "Amor"

The historic life of mankind began with the confusion of Babel (Gen. 11); it will end in the perfect harmony of the new Jerusalem (Rev. 21). Between these two extreme limits, described in the first and last books of Scripture, takes place the evolution of universal history of which a symbolic representation is given us in the sacred book which may be regarded as transitional between the Old and New Testaments, the book of the prophet Daniel (Dan. 2:31–36).

Since mankind on earth is not, and was never meant to be, a world of pure spirits, it needs for the expression and development of the unity of its inner life an external social organism which must become more centralized as it grows in extent and diversity. Just as the life of the individual human soul manifests itself by means of the organized human body, so the collective soul of regenerate humanity, the invisible Church, requires a visible social organism as the symbol and instrument of its unity.

From this point of view, the history of mankind presents itself as the gradual formation of a universal social entity or of the one Catholic Church in the broadest sense of the term. This work is inevitably divided into two main parts: 1) the outward unification of the nations of history, or the formation of the universal *body* of mankind by the efforts, more or less unconscious, of earthly powers under the invisible and indirect action of Providence, and 2) the vivifying of this body by the mighty breath of the God-Man and its further development by the combined action of divine grace and more or less conscious human forces.

In other words, we have here on the one hand the formation of natural universal monarchy, and on the other the formation and development of spiritual monarchy or the universal Church on the basis and in the framework of the corresponding natural organism. The first part of this great work constitutes the essence of ancient or pagan history; the second part mainly determines modern or Christian history. The connecting link is the history of the people of Israel who, under the active guidance of the living God, prepared the setting, both organic and national, for the appearance of the God-Man who is both the spiritual principle of unity for the universal body and the absolute center of history.

While the chosen nation was preparing the natural body of the individual God-Man, the Gentile nations were evolving the social body of the collective God-Man, the universal Church. And since this task allotted to paganism was achieved by purely human efforts guided only indirectly and invisibly by divine Providence, it was bound to proceed by a series of attempts and experiments. Previous to any effective universal monarchy, we see the rise of various national monarchies claiming universality but incapable of achieving it.

After the Assyrio-Babylonian monarchy, the head of gold, denoting the purest and most concentrated despotism, comes the monarchy of the Medes and Persians represented by the breast and arms of silver, which symbolize a less unmitigated, less concentrated, but on the other hand much more extensive despotism, embracing the whole scene of contemporary history from Greece on the one side to India on the other.

Next comes the Macedonian monarchy of Alexander the Great, the brazen belly engulfing Hellas and the East. Despite the fruitfulness of Hellenism in the sphere of intellectual and aesthetic culture, it proved impotent in practical affairs and incapable of creating a political framework or a center of unity for the vast multitude of nations which it penetrated. In administration it took over, without any essential alteration, the absolutism of the national despots which it found in the East; and though it imposed the unity of its culture on the world which it conquered, it could not prevent that world from splitting into two great semi-Hellenized national states, the Helleno-Egyptian kingdom of the Ptolemies and the Helleno-Syrian kingdom of the Seleucids. These two kingdoms, at one moment engaged in bitter warfare, at another precariously allied by dynastic marriages, were well symbolized by the two feet of the colossus in which the iron of primitive despotism was mingled with the soft clay of a decadent culture.

Thus the pagan world, divided between two rival powers, with Alexandria and Antioch as their two political and intellectual centers, could not provide an adequate historic basis for Christian unity. But there was a stone, a little Italian town, whose origin was hidden among mysterious legends and prophetic portents, and even whose real name was unknown. This stone, hurled forth by the Providence of the God of history, smote the feet of clay of the Greco-barbarian world of the East, overthrew and crushed to powder the impotent colossus, and became a great mountain. The pagan world was given a real center of unity. A truly international and universal monarchy was established, embracing both East and West. Not only was it far more extensive than the greatest of the national monarchies, not only did it include far more heterogeneous national and cultural elements, but it was above all powerfully centralized, and it transformed these varied elements into a positive, active whole. Instead of a monstrous image made up of heterogeneous parts, mankind became an organized and homogeneous body, the Roman Empire, with an individual living center in Caesar Augustus, the trustee and representative of the united will of mankind.

But who was this Caesar and how had he come to represent the living center of humanity? On what was his power based? Long and painful experience had convinced the nations of East and West that continual strife and division were a curse and that some center of unity was essential to the peace of the world. This vague but very real desire for peace and unity threw the pagan world at the feet of an adventurer who succeeded in replacing beliefs and principles by the weapons of his legions and his own personal courage. Thus the unity of the empire was based solely on force and chance. Though the first of the Caesars seemed to deserve his fortune by his personal genius, and the second justified his to a certain extent by his calculated piety and wise moderation, the third was a monster and was succeeded by idiots and madmen. The universal state, which should have been the social incarnation of reason itself, took shape in an absolutely irrational phenomenon, the absurdity of which was only heightened by the blasphemy of the emperor's apotheosis.

The divine Word, individually united to human nature and desiring to unite socially with himself the collective being of man, could not take either the confusion of an anarchic mass of nations or the autocracy of a tyrant as the starting point of this union. He could only unite human society with himself by means of a power founded upon truth.

In the social sphere we are not directly and primarily concerned with personal virtues and defects. We believe the imperial power of pagan Rome to have been evil and false, not merely because of the crimes and follies of a Tiberius or a Nero, but mainly because, whether represented by Caligula or Antonine, it was itself based on violence and crowned with falsehood. The actual emperor, the momentary creature of the praetorians and the legionaries, only owed his power to crude, blind force; the ideal, deified emperor was an impious fiction.

Against the false man-god of political monarchy the true God-Man set up the spiritual power of ecclesiastical monarchy founded on truth and love. Universal monarchy and international unity were to remain; the center of unity was to keep its place. But the central power itself, its character, its origin, and its authority— all this was to be renewed.

The Romans themselves had a vague presentiment of this mysterious transformation. While the ordinary name of Rome was the Greek word for "might," the citizens of the Eternal City believed that they discovered the true meaning of her name by reading it backward in Semitic fashion: *amor*; and the ancient legend revived by Virgil connected the Roman people and the dynasty of Caesar in particular with the mother of love, and through her with the supreme God. But their love was the servant of death and their supreme god was a parricide. The piety of the Romans, which is their chief claim to glory and the foundation of their greatness, was a true sentiment though rooted in a false principle, and it was just that change of principle that was necessary in order that the true Rome might be revealed based upon the true religion. The countless triads of parricidal gods must be replaced by the single divine Trinity, consubstantial and indivisible, and the universal society of mankind must be set up, not on the basis of an empire of might, but on that of a Church of love.

Was it a mere coincidence that, when Jesus Christ wished to announce the foundation of his true universal monarchy, not upon the servile submission of its subjects or upon the autocracy of a human ruler, but upon the free surrender of men's faith and love to God's truth and grace, he chose for that pronouncement the moment of his arrival with his disciples at the outskirts of Caesarea Philippi, the town which a slave of the Caesars had dedicated to the genius of his master? Or again was it a coincidence that Jesus chose the neighborhood of the Sea of Tiberias for the giving of the final sanction to that which he had founded, and that, under the shadow of those monuments which spoke of the actual ruler of false Rome, he consecrated the future ruler of true Rome in words which indicated both the mystical name of the Eternal City and the supreme principle of his new kingdom: "Simon, son of John, do you *love* me more than these?" (John 21:15).

But why must true love, which knows no envy and whose unity implies no exclusiveness, be centered in a single individual and assume for its operation in society the form of monarchy in preference to all others? Since here it is not a question of the omnipotence of God, which might impose truth and justice upon men from without, but rather of the divine love in which man shares by a free act of adherence, the direct action of the Godhead must be reduced to a minimum. It cannot be entirely suppressed, however, since all men are false and no human entity, either individual or collective, left to its own resources, can maintain itself in a constant and progressive relationship to the Godhead. The fruitful love of God, however—united to divine wisdom in order to assist human weakness, while at the same time allowing human forces full play—chooses the path. It is the path along which the unifying and life-giving action of supernatural truth and grace on the mass of mankind will encounter the fewest natural obstacles and will find a social framework externally conformable and adapted to the manifestation of true unity; and the path which facilitates union between the divine and the human in the social order by forming a central, unifying organ within humanity itself is the path of monarchy. The creation afresh of a spontaneous unity on the chaotic basis of independent opinions and conflicting wills would otherwise require a new, direct, and manifestly miraculous intervention of the Godhead each time, an activity out of nothing forced upon men and depriving them of their moral freedom. As the divine Word did not appear upon earth in his heavenly splendor but in the lowliness of human nature, as today he assumes the lowly appearance of material "species" in order to give himself to the faithful, so it is not his will to rule human society directly by his divine power but to employ as the normal instrument of his social activity a form of unity already in existence among men, namely, universal monarchy.

It was necessary, however, to regenerate, spiritualize, and sanctify this social form by substituting the eternal principle of grace and truth for the mortal principle of violence and deception; to replace the head of an army, who in the spirit of falsehood declared himself to be a god, with the head of all the faithful, who in the spirit of truth recognized and acknowledged in his Master the Son of the living God; to dethrone a raving despot who would willingly have enslaved the human race and drained the blood of his victim, and to raise up in his place the loving servant of a God who shed his blood for mankind.

Within the borders of Caesarea and on the shores of the Sea of Tiberias, Jesus dethroned Caesar—not the Caesar of the tribute-money or the Christian Caesar of the future, but the deified Caesar, the sole, absolute, and independent sovereign of the universe, the supreme center of unity for the human race. He dethroned him because he had created a new and better center of unity, a new and better sovereign power based upon faith and love, truth and grace. And while dethroning the false and impious absolutism of the pagan Caesars, Jesus confirmed and made eternal the universal monarchy of Rome by giving it its true theocratic basis. It was in a certain sense nothing more than a change of dynasty; the dynasty of Julius Caesar, supreme pontiff and god, gave place to the dynasty of Simon Peter, supreme pontiff and servant of the servants of God.

Chapter 8

The "Son of Man" and the "Rock"

The interpretation given in our last chapter helps to explain why the prophetic vision of the great pagan powers, which is as complete and exact as such a vision could be, makes no mention of the greatest power of all, the Roman Empire. That is because this empire was not a part of the monstrous colossus doomed to destruction but was the abiding material framework and mold of the kingdom of God. The great powers of the ancient world were merely passing figures upon the stage of history; Rome alone lives forever. The rock of the capitol was hallowed by the stone of the Bible, and the Roman Empire was transformed into the great mountain which in the prophetic vision sprang from that stone. And what can that stone itself mean except the monarchical power of him who was called the rock par excellence and on whom the universal Church, the mountain of God, was founded?

The image of this mysterious stone in the book of Daniel is usually applied to Jesus Christ himself. It is noteworthy, however, that though Jesus made considerable use of the prophet Daniel in his preaching, he did not, in speaking of his own person, borrow from the prophet the symbol of the stone, but another title which he used almost as his own name: the Son of Man. He employs this very name in the crucial passage of Matthew: " 'Who do men say that the Son of Man is?' " (Matt. 16:13). Jesus is the Son of Man seen by the prophet Daniel (Dan. 7:13), whereas the stone (Dan. 2:34, 35, 45) does not directly denote Jesus, but the fundamental authority of the Church, and the Son of Man himself applies this symbol to its first representative: "And I tell you, you are Peter" (Matt. 16:18).

The context of the prophecy of Daniel directly confirms our view, for it speaks of a kingdom coming from God but nevertheless visible and earthly, destined to conquer, destroy, and replace the great pagan empires. The appearance and triumph of this fifth kingdom, which in a parallel passage is called "the people of the saints of the Most High" (Dan. 7:18, 27) and which is obviously the universal Church, are symbolically represented by this stone which, after breaking the feet of the colossus, becomes a great mountain and fills the whole earth.

If, then, the stone mentioned by Daniel directly denoted Christ, it would follow that it was Christ himself who became the "great mountain," or, in other words, the universal monarchy of the Church, to which the pagan empires gave place. But why should we go out of our way to attribute to the truly inspired author of this wonderful book such confused and incongruous imagery, when all the while a clear and harmonious interpretation is not only open to us but is absolutely forced upon us by the comparison between these prophetic passages and the corresponding passage of the Gospel?

Both in Daniel and in Matthew we find the Son of Man and the rock of the Church. Now, it is absolutely certain that the Son of Man, whether in the prophetic book or in the Gospel, denotes one and the same person, the Messiah; the analogy demands therefore that the rock of the Church bears the same sense in both passages. But in the Gospel, the rock is obviously the prince of the apostles —*tu es Petrus* ["you are Peter"]; hence the "stone" of the prophet Daniel must equally foreshadow the original trustee of monarchical authority in the universal Church, the rock which was taken and hurled, not by human hands, but by the Son of the living God and by the heavenly Father himself, revealing to the supreme ruler of the Church that divine-human truth which is the source of his authority.

There is a further remarkable coincidence to be noted. The great king of Babylon, the typical representative of false universal monarchy, saw in a mysterious dream the chief representative of true universal monarchy under the significant image of a stone which was to become his actual name. Moreover, he saw the complete contrast between the two monarchies: the one beginning in the head of gold and ending in feet of clay which crumble to dust, the other beginning in a little stone and ending in a huge mountain which fills the world.

Chapter 9

Ancient and Modern Witness
to the Primacy of Peter

"Granted that Jesus Christ established in the person of Peter a central sovereign authority over the Church; it is still not clear how and for what purpose this authority could have passed to the Roman Church and the papacy." This is the reply which sincere Orthodox have been compelled by the evidence to make to us. In other words, they admit that no human hand shaped the stone, but they shut their eyes to the great mountain which has grown out of it. Yet the phenomenon is amply explained in Scripture by similes and parables which are familiar to everyone, though none the better understood for all that.

Though the transformation of a stone into a mountain is only a symbol, the transformation of a simple, almost imperceptible seed into an infinitely larger and more complicated organism is an actual fact. And it is by just this fact that the New Testament foretells and illustrates the development of the Church, as of a great tree which began in an imperceptible grain of seed and to-day gives ample shelter to the beasts of the field and the fowls of the air.

Now, even among Catholics we meet with ultradogmatic spirits who, while justly admiring the vast oak tree which covers them with its shade, absolutely refuse to admit that all this abundance of organic forms has grown from a structure as simple and rudimentary as that of an ordinary acorn. According to them, though the oak arose out of the acorn, the acorn must have contained in a distinct and discernible form, if not every leaf, at least every

149

branch of the great tree, and must have been not only identical in substance with the latter but similar to it in every detail.

Whereupon ultracritical spirits of the opposite school set to work to examine the wretched acorn minutely from every angle. Naturally, they discover in it no resemblance whatever to the entwining roots, the stout trunk, the leafy branches, or the tough, corrugated foliage of the great tree. "What humbug," they exclaim. "The acorn is simply an acorn and can never be anything else; it is only too obvious where the great oak and all its characteristics came from. The Jesuits invented it at the [First] Vatican Council; we saw it with our own eyes—in the book of Janus."[1]

At the risk of appearing a freethinker to the extreme dogmatists and of being at the same time labeled a Jesuit in disguise by the critics, I must affirm the unquestionable truth that the acorn actually has a quite simple and rudimentary structure, and that though not all the component parts of a great oak can be discovered in it, the oak has actually grown out of the acorn without any artificial stimulus or infringement of the laws of nature, but by its own right, nay, even by divine right. Since God, who is not bound by the limitations of time and space and of the mechanism of the material world, sees concealed in the actual seeds of things all their future potentialities, so in the little acorn he must not only have seen but ordained and blessed the mighty oak which was to grow from it. In the grain of mustard seed of Peter's faith he discerned and foretold the vast tree of the Catholic Church which was to cover the earth with its branches.

Though Jesus Christ entrusted Peter with that universal sovereign authority which was to endure and develop within the Church throughout its existence upon earth, he did not personally exercise this authority except in a measure and in a form suited to the primitive condition of the apostolic Church. The action

---

[1] Under the pseudonym of "Janus," Ignaz von Dollinger and others wrote a series of open letters in 1869, trying to forestall the [First] Vatican Council's pronouncement on papal infallibility.—ED.

of the prince of the apostles had as little resemblance to modern papal administration as the acorn has to the oak; but this does not prevent the papacy from being the natural, logical, and legitimate development of the primacy of Peter. The primacy itself is so marked in the historical books of the New Testament that no theologian of good faith, whether Orthodox, rationalist, or Jew,[2] has ever disputed it. We have already cited the eminent Jewish writer Joseph Salvador as an unbiased witness to the historical foundation of the Church by Jesus Christ and to the outstanding part allotted to Peter in its foundation. A writer equally free from Catholic bias, David Strauss, the well-known leader of the German school of critics, has found himself compelled to defend the primacy of Peter against Protestant controversialists whom he accuses of prejudice.[3]

As regards the representatives of Eastern Orthodoxy, we cannot do better than to quote once more our one and only theologian, Philaret of Moscow. For him the primacy of Peter is "clear and evident."[4] After recalling that Christ entrusted Peter with the special task of confirming his brethren (Luke 22:32), that is to say, the other apostles, the famous Russian prelate continues thus:

> In point of fact, although the Resurrection of our Lord had been announced to the women who came bearing spices, this did not confirm the apostles in their faith in the event (Luke 24:11). But when the risen Lord had appeared to Peter, the other apostles (even before the appearance to them all together) declared with conviction: "The Lord has risen indeed, and has appeared to Simon" (Luke 24:34). Finally, when it is a question of filling the gap left in the apostolic band by the apostasy of Judas, it is Peter who is the first to draw attention to the fact and to take the decisive step; when the moment arrives, just after the descent of the Holy Spirit,

---

[2] The same sincerity is not usually found in Protestant writers. The best among them, however, admit the fact of the primacy, though they make fruitless attempts to interpret it according to their liking.

[3] *Vie de Jésus* [*Life of Jesus*] (tr. Littre, Paris, 1839), 1:2:584; cf. 378.

[4] *Sermons and Addresses of Philaret, Metropolitan of Moscow* (1873, etc.), 2:214.

for the solemn inauguration of the preaching of the gospel, "Peter,
standing up . . ."; when the foundations of the Christian Church
are to be laid among pagans as well as among Jews, it is Peter who
gives Cornelius baptism and thus, not for the first time, fulfills the
utterance of Christ: "You are Peter," etc.[5]

In bearing this witness to the truth, the eloquent doctor of the
modern Russian church is but the echo of the still more eloquent
Doctor of the ancient Greek church. John Chrysostom long ago
anticipated and triumphantly refuted the objections to the primacy of Peter which are made even today on the ground of certain incidents in the record of the Gospel and of the apostolic
Church, such as Simon's denial in the high priest's palace, his
dealings with Paul, and so forth. We refer our Orthodox readers
to the arguments of the great Ecumenical Doctor.[6] No Roman
Catholic could assert more forcibly and insistently the primacy of
power (and not merely of honor) which belonged to Peter in the
apostolic Church. The prince of the apostles, to whose care all
were committed by Christ, had, according to this saintly writer,
the power of nominating a successor to Judas on his own authority, and if on this occasion he called in the assistance of the other
apostles it was by no means of obligation, but simply of his good
pleasure that he did so.[7]

Scripture tells us of the primacy of Peter; his right to absolute
sovereign authority in the Church is attested by Orthodox tradition; but no one possessed of any historical feeling or indeed
of any ordinary common sense would expect to find legally defined powers taking effect according to fixed rules in the primitive
Church, not only of the period when "the multitude of believers

---

[5] Ibid.

[6] The Greco-Russian church, as is well known, specially attributes this title
to three ancient Fathers: St. Basil of Caesarea, surnamed the Great, St. Gregory
Nazianzen, surnamed the Theologian, and St. John Chrysostom. They have
a feast in common on January 30 in our calendar.

[7] *Works*, 9:27, 30–31.

had but one heart and one soul" but also long after. There is always the temptation to expect to find the branches of the oak in the acorn. The real and living seed of the supreme authority of the Church which we discern in the prince of the apostles could only be displayed in the primitive Church by practical leadership on the part of Peter in every matter which concerned the universal Church, and this is what we actually find in the Gospels and the Acts of the Apostles.[8]

Since there are actually critics who do not recognize the personality of Paul in his epistles, there will always be some who will not observe the outstanding part played by Peter in the foundation of the Church. We will not stay longer to refute them, but will pass on to the objection raised against the succession of Rome to the position of the Galilean fisherman.

---

[8] Those of our Orthodox readers who find neither the authority of saintly Fathers such as John Chrysostom nor that of Russian theologians such as Archbishop Philaret sufficient to convince them of Peter's unique place in New Testament history will perhaps be amenable to what may be called statistical proof. Since it occurred to me that none of Jesus' intimate disciples had so considerable a claim to a prominent place as St. John, the beloved apostle, I counted up the number of times that John and Peter are mentioned respectively in the Gospels and in Acts, and found the proportion to be about 1 to 4. Peter is mentioned by name 171 times (114 times in the Gospels and 57 times in Acts), John only 46 times (38 times in the Gospels, including the instances where he refers to himself indirectly, and 8 times in Acts).

Chapter 10

The Apostle Peter and the Papacy

"The apostle Peter possesses the primacy of power; but why should the pope of Rome succeed to this primacy?" We must confess our entire inability to understand how such a question can be taken seriously. Once it is admitted that there is in the universal Church a fundamental supreme authority established by Christ in the person of Peter, then it must follow that this authority is in existence somewhere. And it seems to us that the obvious impossibility of discovering it anywhere else but at Rome is at once a sufficient reason for supporting the Catholic contention.

Since neither the patriarch of Constantinople nor the Synod of St. Petersburg claims or can possibly claim to represent the rock of the universal Church, that is to say, the real and fundamental unity of ecclesiastical authority, there is no choice but either to abandon any notion of such a unity and accept a state of division, confusion, and bondage as the normal condition of the Church, or else to acknowledge the claims and actual validity of the one and only existing authority which has always shown itself to be the center of ecclesiastical unity.

No amount of argument can overcome the evidence for the fact that apart from Rome there only exist national churches such as the Armenian or the Greek church, state churches such as the Russian or Anglican, or else sects founded by individuals, such as the Lutherans, the Calvinists, the Irvingites [the Catholic Apostolic church], and so forth. The Roman Catholic Church is the only church that is neither a national church, nor a state church, nor a sect founded by a man; it is the only church in the world which maintains and asserts the principle of universal social unity against individual egoism and national particularism; it is the only church which maintains and asserts the freedom of the spiritual power against the absolutism of the state; in a word, it is the only church against which the gates of Hades have not prevailed.

"Thus you will know them by their fruits" (Matt. 7:20). In the sphere of religious fellowship, the fruit of Catholicism (for those who have remained Catholics) is the unity and freedom of the Church; the fruit of Protestantism for its adherents both in the East and in the West is division and bondage: division chiefly in the West and bondage in the East. Think and say what you will of the Roman Church or of the papacy; we ourselves are very far from seeing or expecting to find in either the achievement of perfection or the realization of the ideal. We are aware that the rock of the Church is not the Church itself, that the foundation is not the same as the building, nor the way the same as the goal.

All that we are maintaining is that the papacy is the sole international and independent ecclesiastical authority, the only real and permanent basis for the Church's universal activity. That is an indisputable fact and in itself compels us to acknowledge the pope to be the sole trustee of those powers and privileges which Peter received from Christ. And since the universal monarchy of the Church was not to eliminate the universal monarchy of the political world but to transubstantiate it, was it not natural that the visible seat of the two corresponding monarchies should remain the same? If, as has already been said, the dynasty of Julius Caesar was in a certain sense to give place to the dynasty of Simon Peter, if Caesarism was to yield to papacy, it was surely to be expected that the papacy should take up its abode in the existing center of the universal empire.

The transference to Rome of the supreme ecclesiastical authority established by Christ in the person of Peter is a patent fact attested to by the tradition of the Church and justified by the logic of circumstances. As regards the question of the formal manner in which the authority of Peter was transmitted to the bishop of Rome, that is a historical problem which for lack of documentary evidence can hardly be solved scientifically.

We believe the Orthodox tradition which is recorded in our liturgical books to the effect that, on his arrival in Rome, Peter definitely fixed his See there and before his death personally nominated his successor. Later times saw the popes elected by the Christian community of the city of Rome until the present mode of election by the college of cardinals was definitely established. Furthermore, as early as the second century we have in the writings of St. Irenaeus unimpeachable evidence that the Church of Rome was already regarded by the whole Christian world as the center of unity, and that the bishop of Rome enjoyed a permanent position of supreme authority, though the forms in which this authority found expression were bound to vary with the times, becoming more definite and imposing in proportion as the development of the whole social structure of the Church became more intricate and diversified.

"In fact" (to quote a historian of the critical rationalist school), "in 196 the chosen heads of the churches were attempting to create ecclesiastical unity; one of them, the head of the Roman Church, seemed to claim the role of executive authority within the community and to assume the position of sovereign pontiff."[1] But it was not merely a question of executive authority, for the same author, a little further on, makes the following admission: "Tertullian and Cyprian appear to hail the Church of Rome as the principal church and in a certain degree the guardian and keeper of the faith and of genuine tradition."[2]

In the early days of Christianity, the monarchical authority of the universal Church was but a seed scarcely visible but nevertheless pregnant with life; by the second century, this seed has visibly developed, as the acts of Pope Victor testify; in the third century, the same witness is borne by the acts of Pope Stephen and Pope Dionysius, and in the fourth by those of Pope Julius I. In

---

[1] B. Aubé, *Les Chrétiens dans l'Empire Romain, de la Fin des Antonins au Milieu du Troisième Siècle* [*Christians in the Roman Empire from the End of the Antonines to the Middle of the Third Century*], 69.

[2] Ibid., 146.

the following century, we already see the supreme authority and monarchical power of the Roman Church growing like a vigorous sapling under Pope St. Leo I; and, finally, by the ninth century the papacy is already the mighty and majestic tree which covers the Christian world with the shadow of its branches.

That is the great fact, the main fact, the manifestation and fulfillment in history of the divine utterance: "You are Peter" (Matt. 16:18). This broad fact is the outcome of divine law, while particular facts regarding the transmission of the sovereign power, the papal elections, and so forth concern the purely human side of the Church and have no more than a secondary interest from the religious point of view. Here again, the Roman Empire, foreshadowing as it does in a certain sense the Roman Church, may provide us with an analogy. Since Rome was the undisputed center of the empire, the individual who was proclaimed emperor at Rome was immediately recognized as such by the whole world without any question as to whether it was the Senate or the praetorians or the votes of the people which had raised him to the purple. In exceptional cases, when the legions outside Rome elected the emperor, his first concern was to hasten to the imperial city. Without its support, everyone would regard his election as only provisional.

The Rome of the popes became for universal Christendom what the Rome of the Caesars had been for the pagan world. The bishop of Rome was by his very office the supreme pastor and doctor of the whole Church. There was no need to trouble about the method of his election; that depended on circumstances and conditions of the moment. There was usually no more reason for doubting the legality of the election of the bishop of Rome than that of the election of any other bishop. And once his election to the episcopate was recognized, the head of the central Church and the occupant of the Chair of Peter was ipso facto in possession of all the rights and powers which Christ conferred upon the rock of the Church.

There were exceptional instances in which doubt might be felt about the election; antipopes are not unknown to history. But just as the usurpers Demetrius and Peter III in no way robbed the Russian monarchy of its lawful authority, so the antipopes provide no argument against the papacy. Any apparent abnormality in the history of the Church belongs to the human "species" rather than to the divine "substance" of the religious society. If by some chance adulterated or even poisoned wine were used in the sacrament of the Eucharist, would this sacrilege have the slightest effect on the validity of the sacrament itself?

In maintaining that the bishop of Rome is the true successor of Peter and therefore the impregnable rock of the Church and the steward of the kingdom of heaven, we are setting aside the question whether the prince of the apostles was ever personally in Rome. This fact is attested by the tradition of the Church both in the East and in the West, and we ourselves feel no doubt in the matter. But if some Christians in good faith are more susceptible than ourselves to the specious arguments of Protestant scholars, we have no wish to dispute the matter with them. We might even admit that Peter never went personally to Rome, and yet at the same time, from the religious point of view, maintain a spiritual and mystical transmission of his sovereign authority to the bishop of the Eternal City.

The history of early Christianity supplies us with a striking instance of an analogous relationship. Paul had no natural link whatever with Jesus Christ; he was not a witness of our Lord's life on earth nor did he receive his commission in any visible or public fashion; all Christians nevertheless recognize him as one of the greatest apostles. His apostolate was a public ministry in the Church, yet its origin, in his relation to Jesus Christ, is a mystical and miraculous fact. Now if a phenomenon of a supernatural order formed the original link between Jesus Christ and Paul and made the latter a chosen vessel and the apostle of the Gentiles, though at the same time this miraculous commission did not prevent his further activity from being subject to the natural conditions of human life and historic circumstances, then, similarly, that original relationship between Peter and the See of Rome which created the papacy might well depend upon a mystical and transcendental

act, which would in no way deprive the papacy itself, once constituted, of the character of a normal social institution acting under
the ordinary conditions of earthly life.

The mighty spirit of Peter, guided by his Master's almighty will,
might well seek to perpetuate the center of ecclesiastical unity by
taking up his abode in the center of the political unity already
formed by Providence, thus making the bishop of Rome heir to
his primacy. According to this theory (which, let us remember,
would become necessary only if it were conclusively shown that
Peter did not go to Rome), the pope would be regarded as the successor of Peter in the same spiritual and yet absolutely real sense in
which, *mutatis mutandis*, Paul must be recognized as a true apostle
chosen and sent by Jesus Christ, though he had no knowledge of
him except in a miraculous vision. The Acts of the Apostles and
the epistles of Paul himself attest to his apostleship; the unbroken
tradition of the universal Church attests to the succession of the
Roman primacy from Peter. For an Orthodox Christian, the latter
evidence is intrinsically of no less value than the former. We might
well be ignorant of the manner in which the foundation rock of
the Church was removed from Palestine to Italy; but that it was
actually so removed and established at Rome is an incontrovertible
fact, the rejection of which would involve the denial not only of
sacred tradition but of the very history of Christianity.

The point of view which ranks fact lower than principle and lays
greater emphasis on a general truth than on the external certainty
of material phenomena is by no means peculiar to ourselves; it
is the opinion of the Orthodox church herself. Let us quote an
example in order to make our meaning clear. It is absolutely certain that the First Ecumenical Council of Nicaea was summoned
by the Emperor Constantine and not by Pope St. Sylvester. Nevertheless, the Greco-Russian church in the office of January 2,
in which she celebrates the memory of Sylvester, has accorded to
him special praise for having summoned the 318 fathers to Nicaea
and promulgated the orthodox dogma against the blasphemy of
Arius.

This is no mere historical error—the history of the first council was well known in the Eastern church—but rather the expression of a general truth far more important for the religious conscience of the Church than material accuracy. Once the primacy of the popes was recognized in principle, it was natural to ascribe to each pope all the ecclesiastical acts that took place during his pontificate. Thus, with the general fundamental rule of the life of the Church in mind rather than the historical details of a particular event, the Easterns assigned to Sylvester the privileges and duties which were his according to the spirit, if not the letter, of Christian history. And if it is true that the letter killeth but the spirit giveth life, they were right.

Chapter 11

St. Leo the Great on the Primacy

This is not the place to set forth the whole historical development of the papacy or to quote the copious testimony borne by Orthodox tradition to the lawfulness of the papal sovereignty in the universal Church. In order to demonstrate the historical basis of our argument to those of our readers who are not familiar with Church history, it will be enough to dwell upon a single epoch, memorable in the history of the papacy, an epoch which is sufficiently primitive to command the respect of our Orthodox traditionalists and which, at the same time, stands revealed in the broad daylight of historical knowledge and documentary evidence, and so presents no obscurity or ambiguity in its essential outlines.

The epoch in question is the middle of the fifth century, the period when the Roman Church had so worthy a representative in Pope St. Leo the Great. It is interesting for us to note the conception that this Roman pontiff—who is also a recognized saint of the Greco-Russian church—had of his own authority, and how his assertions were received in the Eastern part of the Church.

In one of his sermons, after reminding his hearers that Christ is the only pontiff in the strict sense of the word, Leo continues thus:

> Now, he has not abandoned the care of his flock; and it is from his supreme and eternal authority that we have received the abundant gift of apostolic power, and his succor is never absent from his work. . . . For that firmness of faith which was commended in the prince of the apostles is perpetual, and as that on which Peter believed in Christ endures, so does that which Christ established

in Peter endure also. . . . The dispensation of the truth therefore abides; and the blessed Peter, persevering in the strength of the rock wherewith he has been endowed, has not abandoned the reins of the Church which he received. . . . Thus if we act or decide justly, if by our daily supplications we obtain anything from the mercy of God, it is the work and the merit of him whose power lives and whose authority prevails in his See.

And speaking of the bishops gathered in Rome for the feast of Peter, Leo says that they have desired to honor by their presence "him whom they know not only to preside in this See [of Rome] but also to be the primate of all the bishops."[1]

In another sermon—after expressing what may be called the fundamental truth of the Church, that in the sphere of the inner life of grace all Christians are priests and kings, but that differences and inequalities are necessary in the outward structure of the mystical body of Christ—Leo goes on to say:

And yet out of the whole world Peter alone is chosen to be set above the assembly of all the nations, above all the apostles and all the Fathers of the Church, to the end that though among God's people there are many priests and many pastors, yet all might be duly governed by Peter, being ultimately governed by Christ. Behold, dearly beloved, how great a share in his own power was bestowed by the will of God upon this man, and if God willed that the rest of the apostles should share anything in common with him, yet it was through him that he bestowed whatever he did not withhold from the others. . . . *And I say unto thee*: that is to say, as my Father has revealed unto thee my Godhead, so I make known to thee thy preeminence; *that thou art Peter*: that is to say, though I am the inviolable rock, though I am the cornerstone who has made both one, though I am the foundation other than which none can be laid, yet thou also art the rock strengthened by my might and so sharing in common with me that which I possess by my own power.[2]

---

[1] *Works* (ed. Migne, Paris, 1846, etc.), 1:145–147.
[2] Ibid., 149.

The power of binding and loosing was handed on to the other apostles also, and through them to all the rulers of the Church; but not for nothing was a single individual entrusted with what belongs to all. . . . Peter is fortified with the strength of all, and the assistance of divine grace is so ordered that the stability bestowed by Christ on Peter is conferred by Peter on the apostles.[3]

As Peter shares in the sovereign authority of Christ over the universal Church, so the bishop of Rome who occupies the See of Peter is the living representative of this authority.

Peter does not cease to preside in his See and his *consortium* with the Eternal Pontiff never fails. For that steadfastness with which he was endowed, when he was first made the rock, by Christ who is himself the rock, has passed to his successors, and wherever any stability is manifest, it is beyond doubt the might of the supreme pastor which is in evidence. Could anyone consider the renown of blessed Peter and yet be ignorant or envious enough to assert that there is any part of the Church which is not guided by his care and strengthened by his succor?[4]

Though every individual pastor tends his flock with a special care and knows that he must give account of the sheep committed to his charge, we alone must nevertheless share the anxiety of all, and our responsibility includes the governance of each individual. For since the whole world has recourse to the See of the blessed apostle Peter, and since that love toward the universal Church which was enjoined upon him by our Lord is expected of our administration also, therefore the greater our responsibility toward all the faithful, the heavier is the burden which weighs upon us.[5]

The renown of Peter is, to Leo's mind, inseparable from the renown of the Roman Church, which he calls "the holy nation, the chosen people, the priestly and royal state, which has become the head of the world through the blessed Peter's Holy See."[6]

---

[3] Ibid., 151–152; cf. 429–432.

[4] Ibid., 155–156.

[5] Ibid., 153.

[6] Ibid., 423.

"He, the chief of the apostolic band, was appointed to the citadel of the Roman Empire that the light of the truth which was being revealed for the salvation of all the nations might spread more effectually from the head itself throughout the whole body of the world."[7]

---

[7] Ibid., 424.

Chapter 12

St. Leo the Great on Papal Authority

Believing as he did that the supreme authority of Peter resided permanently in the Roman Church, Leo the Great could not regard himself otherwise than as "the ruler of the Christian world,"[1] responsible for the peace and good order of all the churches.[2] Constant attention to this huge task was for him a religious obligation. "The demands of religious duty (*ratio pietatis*)," he writes to the African bishops, "require that we should make every effort to ascertain the exact state of affairs with that solicitude which, according to the divine command, we owe to the universal Church. . . . For the stability and order of the Lord's whole household would be disturbed if there were lacking in the head anything of which the body had need."[3]

The same ideas are found expressed in a more developed form in his letter to the bishops of Sicily:

> We are urged by divine precepts and apostolic exhortations to keep a loving and active watch over the state of all the churches, and if there is anything deserving of blame we must be diligent to warn the culprit either against the rashness of ignorance or the presumption of self-aggrandizement. Constrained by the Lord's utterance which urged upon blessed Peter the mystical injunction thrice repeated that he who loves Christ should feed Christ's sheep, we are bound by reverence for his See, which by the abundance of divine grace we occupy, to avoid the peril of sloth so far as we may, lest the

---

[1] The designation given him in the constitution of the Emperor Valentinian III; see *Works*, 1:637.

[2] Ibid., 664.

[3] Ibid., 646.

confession of the holy apostle, whereby he declared himself the Lord's disciple, be required of us in vain. For he who is negligent in feeding the flock so repeatedly entrusted to him is proved to have no love for the Chief Shepherd.[4]

In his letter to St. Flavian, the patriarch of Constantinople, the Pope assigns to himself the task of preserving the Catholic faith intact by cutting off all dissensions, of warning by his own authority (*nostra auctoritate*) the champions of error, and of fortifying those whose faith is approved.[5]

When the Emperor Theodosius II attempted to plead with Leo on behalf of the Archimandrite Eutyches (who was the author of the Monophysite heresy), the sovereign pontiff replied that Eutyches could secure pardon if he recanted the opinions condemned by the Pope, with whom lay the final decision in questions of dogma. "What the Catholic Church believes and teaches on the mystery of the Lord's Incarnation is contained fully in the letter sent to my brother and fellow-bishop Flavian."[6]

Leo did not admit that the ecumenical council had any power of decision on a dogma already defined by the Pope.[7] In the instructions which the Pope gives to his legate, Bishop Paschasinus, he points to his dogmatic letter to Flavian as the complete and final definition of the true faith.[8] In another letter to the Emperor Marcian, Leo declares himself instructed by the Spirit of God to teach and impart the true Catholic faith.[9] In a third letter to the emperor, he states that he has only asked for the summoning of a council in order to restore peace in the Eastern church,[10] and in the letter addressed to the council itself he says that he only accepts it "so that the rights and dignity belonging to the See of

---

[4] Ibid., 695–696.

[5] Ibid., 733.

[6] Ibid., 783.

[7] Ibid., 918; letter to the Emperor Marcian.

[8] Ibid., 927.

[9] Ibid., 930.

[10] Ibid., 932.

the blessed apostle Peter be respected," and he urges the Eastern bishops "to abstain entirely from the rashness of impugning the divinely inspired faith" as he has defined it in his dogmatic epistle. "It is not permitted," he writes,

> to defend that which it is not permitted to believe, since in our letters sent to Bishop Flavian of blessed memory we have already with the greatest fullness and lucidity expounded the true and pure faith concerning the mystery of the Incarnation of our Lord Jesus Christ in accordance with the authoritative record of the Gospels, the words of the prophets, and the teaching of the apostles.[11]

And in the following words, Leo informs the Gaulish bishops of the result of the Council of Chalcedon: "The holy synod, adhering with religious unanimity to that which had been written by our unworthy hand and reinforced by the authority and merit of my lord, the blessed apostle Peter, has cut off from the Church of God this shameful abomination" (the heresy of Eutyches and Dioscorus).[12]

But it is well known that, besides this result which the Pope approved, the Council of Chalcedon was marked by an act of a different kind. In an irregular session, the Eastern bishops subject to the patriarch of Constantinople promulgated the famous twenty-eighth canon, by which they conferred upon their metropolitan the primacy of the East to the prejudice of the patriarchs of Alexandria and Antioch. It is true that they themselves declared the canon to be provisional and humbly submitted it to Leo's judgment, but he repudiated it with indignation and seized this fresh opportunity to define his conception of the hierarchy and the extent of his own authority.

In his letter to the emperor, he observes in the first place that the claims of the patriarch of Constantinople are based upon political considerations and have nothing in common with the primacy of Peter, which is of divine institution.

---

[11] Ibid., 937–939.
[12] Ibid., 987.

Secular things stand upon a different footing from things divine; and no building can be stable apart from the one rock which the Lord has laid for a foundation. . . . Let it suffice him (the Patriarch Anatolius) that he has obtained the bishopric of so great a city with the aid of your piety and the support of my favor. He should not disdain the royal city, even though he cannot change it into an apostolic see; and let him on no account hope to succeed in exalting his own position at the expense of others. . . . Let him remember that it is to me that the government of the Church has been entrusted. I should be responsible if the rules of the Church were infringed through my acquiescence (far be it from me!) or if the will of a single brother had more weight with me than the common good of the Lord's whole house. [13]

"The agreements of the bishops which are contrary to the holy canons of Nicaea . . . we declare to be null and void, and by the authority of the blessed apostle Peter we annul them completely by a general decree." [14]

In his reply to the petition of the bishops of the fourth council, the Pope confirms his approval of their dogmatic decree (formulated on the lines of his own letter to Flavian) as well as his annulment of the twenty-eighth canon. "Your Holiness will be able," he writes, "to appreciate the reverence with which the Apostolic See observes the rules of the holy fathers, by reading my writings in which I have rejected the claims of the bishop of Constantinople; and you will understand that I am, with the help of the Lord, the guardian of the Catholic faith and of the decrees of the fathers." [15]

Leo, as we have just seen, did not think an ecumenical council necessary in the interests of dogmatic truth after the definitions contained in his letter, yet he considered it very desirable for the peace of the Church; and the spontaneous and unanimous adherence of the council to his decrees filled him with joy. He saw in such a voluntary unity the ideal relationship within the hierarchy.

---

[13] Ibid., 995.
[14] Ibid., 1000.
[15] Ibid., 1027ff.

"The merit of the priestly office," he writes to Theodoret, bishop of Cyrus, "gains great luster where the authority of those in command is so maintained that the liberty of those under obedience appears in no way diminished."[16]

> The Lord has not allowed us to suffer harm in the person of our brethren, but what he had already laid down through our ministry he subsequently confirmed by the irrevocable assent of the whole brotherhood to show that it was indeed from himself that "the dogmatic act" proceeded. It was first promulgated by the chief of all sees and then received by the judgment of the whole Christian world so that in this also the members might be in agreement with the head.[17]

The learned Theodoret, as is well known, had been accused of Nestorianism but had been exculpated at the Council of Chalcedon; he himself, however, regarded this judgment as only provisional and applied to the Pope for a final decision. Leo pronounced him orthodox "in the name of our blessed God whose invincible truth has shown thee to be clean from all stain of heresy according to the judgment of the Apostolic See," and he adds: "We acknowledge the exceeding care for us all of blessed Peter, who not only has confirmed the judgment of his See in the definition of the faith, but has also vindicated those who were unjustly condemned."[18]

While he recognized in voluntary agreement the ideal of ecclesiastical unity, in this unity Leo clearly distinguished the element of authority from the element of deliberation, the decision of the Holy See from the consent of the ecumenical council. The ideal of the Church requires such consent on the part of the whole brotherhood; the life of the Church is incomplete without an entire unanimity; but even this universal consent has no real basis and can produce no result without the decisive action of the central authority, as the history of the Church abundantly proves. The

---

[16] Ibid., 1048.
[17] Ibid., 1046–1047.
[18] Ibid., 1053.

last word in all questions of dogma and the final confirmation of every ecclesiastical act belongs to the See of Peter.

Hence in his letter to Anatolius, the patriarch of Constantinople, regarding a cleric of that city, Atticus, who was to recant his heretical opinions and submit himself to the judgment of the fourth council, Leo draws an essential distinction between his own part in the decisions of the ecumenical council and the part played by the Greek patriarch: "He [i.e., Atticus] must promise to maintain in all points the definition of faith of the Council of Chalcedon to which your charity has assented and subscribed and which has been confirmed by the authority of the Apostolic See."[19]

The fundamental principle of Church government could not be better formulated than by drawing Leo's distinction between the authority which confirms and the charity which assents. It is assuredly no mere primacy of honor that the Pope claims in these words. On the contrary, Leo allows a complete equality of honor among all bishops; from that point of view, all were for him brethren and fellow bishops. It was, on the other hand, the distinction of power which he explicitly asserted. The brotherhood of all does not exclude for him the authority of one.

In a letter to Anastasius, bishop of Salonica, on certain matters which "have been entrusted to his brotherly care by the authority of the blessed apostle Peter,"[20] he sums up the conception of the hierarchical principle thus:

> Even among the blessed apostles, there was side by side with an equality of honor a distinction of authority; and though all were equally chosen, preeminence was nevertheless given to one over the others. On the same principle, distinction is made between bishops, and the mighty design of Providence has ordered it that all may not claim every prerogative, but that in each province there should be someone possessing primacy of jurisdiction (literally, "prime judgment") over his brethren; and again, that those presiding in

---

[19] Ibid., 1147.
[20] Ibid., 668.

the larger cities should receive a wider responsibility, that through them the care of the universal Church might ultimately rest upon the one See of Peter and that no part should anywhere be separated from the head.[21]

The ultimate warrant and sanction of this "mighty design of Providence" consists, according to Leo, in the fact that the one head of the Church, with whom the rights and obligations of all are bound up, does not owe his power to the ordinance of man or to the accidents of history, but represents the impregnable rock of truth and justice laid down by the Lord himself as the foundation of his social structure. It is no mere consideration of expediency but the *ratio pietatis* which is invoked by him who has received the government of the whole Church *ex divina institutione* [by divine institution].[22]

---

[21] Ibid., 676.
[22] Ibid., 646.

Chapter 13

The Approval of Leo's Ideas by the Greek Fathers.
The "Robber-Council" of Ephesus

In the writings and acts of Leo I, we see no longer the seed of the sovereign papacy, but the papacy itself, exhibiting the full extent of its powers. To mention only the most important point, the doctrine of infallibility ex cathedra is here proclaimed fourteen centuries before Pius IX. Leo asserts that the authority of Peter's Chair is of itself sufficient to resolve a fundamental question of dogma, and he does not ask the ecumenical council to define the dogma but to assent, for the sake of the peace of the Church, to the definition given by the pope, who is by divine right the lawful guardian of the true Catholic faith. If this thesis, which was merely developed by the [First] Vatican Council in its *Constitutio Dogmatica de Ecclesia Christi*,[1] is a heresy as our own theologians have claimed, then Pope Leo the Great is a declared heretic or rather a heresiarch, since never before had this thesis been affirmed so explicitly, so forcibly, or so insistently.

Let us see, then, the kind of reception the Orthodox church gave to the authoritative assertions of Pope Leo. For this purpose, we will take the acts of those Greek councils which were contemporary with this Pope and read the documents.[2]

We find, first of all, a remarkable letter from Bishop Peter Chrysologus to the Archimandrite Eutyches. When Flavian (the patriarch of Constantinople) had, in conjunction with his synod, condemned Eutyches (archimandrite of one of the monasteries of

---

[1] *Dogmatic Constitution on the Church of Christ.*—ED.

[2] Mansi, *Sacrorum Conciliorum*, vols. v, vi, and vii.

the Greek capital) for heresy, and had applied to the Pope for confirmation of the sentence, Eutyches, following the advice given him at the emperor's court—where he had many influential patrons—attempted to win certain orthodox bishops to his side.

The following is the reply he received from one of them, Peter Chrysologus:

> Above all we advise you, venerable brother, to adhere with the greatest confidence to the writings of the blessed pope of the city of Rome, since the blessed apostle Peter who lives and presides in his own See gives to those who seek it the truth of the faith. As for us, our anxiety for peace and for the faith forbids us to decide causes which concern religion without the assent of the bishop of Rome.[3]

Peter Chrysologus, though a Greek and writing to a Greek, was nevertheless bishop of Ravenna and therefore half Western. But a few pages further on, we find the same doctrine from the representative of the metropolis of the East, Flavian, a saint and confessor of the Orthodox church. On the heresy of Eutyches, he writes thus to the Pope: "The whole question needs only your single decision and all will be settled in peace and quietness. Your sacred letter will with God's help completely suppress the heresy which has arisen and the disturbance which it has caused;[4] and so," he continues, "the convening of a council, which is in any case difficult, will be rendered superfluous."

The learned bishop of Cyrus, Theodoret, whom the Greek church has beatified, should be quoted next to the saintly patriarch of Constantinople:

"If Paul, the herald of the truth and the trumpet of the Holy Spirit," he writes to Pope Leo,

> had recourse to the great Peter . . . we, simple and humble as we are, ought all the more to hasten to your apostolic throne to receive at your hands healing for the wounds which afflict the churches. For

---

[3] Ibid., 5:1349.
[4] Ibid., 1356.

the primacy belongs to you for every reason. Your See is adorned with every sort of privilege, and above all with that of faith, to which the divine apostle bears sufficient witness when, in addressing the Church of Rome, he exclaims: "Your faith is proclaimed in all the world" (Rom. 1:8). . . . It is your See which possesses the tombs of the fathers and doctors of the truth, Peter and Paul, enlightening the souls of the faithful. That divine and thrice-blessed pair appeared in the East and shed their rays abroad; but it was in the West that they chose to be delivered from this life, and it is from thence that they now illumine the whole world. They have shed manifest luster upon your throne, and that is the crown of your blessings.[5]

"As for me, I have only to await the sentence of your Apostolic See. And I beg and beseech Your Holiness to give me, who am unjustly accused, access to your lawful and just tribunal; give but the word and I hasten to receive from you my doctrine in which I have only desired to follow in the apostles' footsteps."[6]

These are no mere empty words or rhetorical phrases addressed to the Pope by the representatives of orthodoxy. The Greek bishops had cause enough to cling to the supreme authority of the Apostolic See. The "robber-council" of Ephesus had just given them ocular demonstration of what an ecumenical council without the pope could be like. It is instructive to recall the circumstances of that occasion.

Since the fourth century, that part of the Church which was mainly Greek in culture had suffered from the rivalry and continual strife of two central sees, the ancient Patriarchate of Alexandria and the new one of Constantinople. The outward fluctuations in this struggle depended mainly on the attitude of the Byzantine court; and if we look into the causes which influenced the attitude of the secular power toward the two ecclesiastical centers of the East, we note a remarkable fact.

From the foregoing, it might be supposed that, from the polit-

---

[5] Ibid., 6:36, 37.
[6] Ibid., 40.

ical point of view, the Byzantine Empire had three lines of action from which to choose: she might support the new Patriarchate of Constantinople as her own creation, always within her control and unable to achieve any permanent independence; or else imperialist Byzantium might wish to avoid the necessity of repressing clericalist tendencies at home and, in order to rid herself of a rather too close and irksome connection, she might prefer to have the center of ecclesiastical administration somewhere farther off and yet within her sphere of influence; she might, with this end in view, be inclined to support the Patriarchate of Alexandria which satisfied both these conditions and in addition could claim, on traditional and canonical grounds, a relative primacy over the East; or lastly, the imperial government might choose to maintain an even balance between the rival sees by favoring now one and now the other according to political circumstances.

It is clear, however, that actually none of these courses was chosen. When ample allowance has been made for individual coincidences or purely personal reactions, it must still be recognized that there was a general motive dictating the policy of the Byzantine emperors in the struggle between the great sees of the East; but the motive lay outside the three political considerations just indicated. If the emperors varied in their attitude toward the two patriarchates, alternately giving first one and then the other their support, this variation had nothing to do with the balance of power; the Byzantine court invariably supported, not the one of the two rival prelates who was least dangerous at the moment, but the one who was in the wrong from the religious or moral point of view.

It was enough for a patriarch, whether of Constantinople or of Alexandria, to be a heretic or an unworthy shepherd of his flock, and he was assured of the active protection of the empire for a considerable period, if not for the rest of his career. And conversely, a saint or a champion of orthodoxy who ascended the episcopal throne either in the city of Alexander or in that of Constantine might count at once upon the hatred and persecution of the imperial court, and often upon nothing short of martyrdom.

This invincible tendency of the Byzantine government toward injustice, violence, and heresy, and its ineradicable antipathy toward the worthiest representatives of the Christian hierarchy, was quick to show itself. Scarcely had the empire recognized the Christian religion than it was already persecuting St. Athanasius, the light of orthodoxy. The whole of the long reign of Constantius, the son of Constantine the Great, was taken up with the struggle against the renowned patriarch of Alexandria, while the emperor backed the heretical bishops of Constantinople. Nor was it the power of the See of Alexandria which was intolerable to the Christian Caesar, but the moral greatness of its occupant.

The position was reversed a half-century later, and the See of Constantinople was occupied by a great saint, John Chrysostom, while the Patriarchate of Alexandria had fallen to Theophilus, a man of the most contemptible character; but the court of Byzantium favored Theophilus and used every means in its power to bring about Chrysostom's downfall. It may be said, however, that it was merely the independent character of the great Christian orator which made him suspect in imperial circles. Yet not long afterward, the church of Constantinople was ruled by Nestorius, a personality of an equally courageous and independent character; but since he possessed the additional qualification of being a determined propagator of heresy, he received every encouragement from Theodosius II and could count on the emperor's unfailing support in his struggle against St. Cyril, the new patriarch of Alexandria and the rival of the great Athanasius, if not in personal character, at least in his zeal for orthodoxy and in his theological ability. We shall see before long why the imperial government did not succeed in upholding the heretic Nestorius and bringing about the fall of Cyril.

Shortly afterward, the position was again reversed: the Patriarchate of Constantinople had in Flavian a worthy successor of John Chrysostom, and the See of Alexandria was now held by a second Theophilus, one Dioscorus, nicknamed "the Pharaoh of Egypt." Flavian was a gentle and unassuming person; Dioscorus' character, on the other hand, was stained with every wickedness and was distinguished mainly by an inordinate ambition and a despotic temper to which he owed his nickname. From the purely political point of view, it was obvious that the imperial government had nothing to fear from Flavian, while the domineering ambitions of the new "pharaoh" might well arouse justifiable apprehensions.

Flavian was orthodox, however, and Dioscorus had the great merit of favoring the new heresy of Monophysitism. That alone was enough to ensure him the support of the Byzantine court,[7] and an ecumenical council was summoned under imperial auspices to give official sanction to his cause. Dioscorus had everything in his favor: the support of the secular arm, a well-disciplined body of clergy brought with him from Egypt and blindly devoted to him, a mob of heretical monks, a considerable following among the clergy of the other patriarchates, and lastly the cowardice of the majority of the orthodox bishops who dared not offer open resistance to a heresy which enjoyed the favor of "the sacred majesty of Divus Augustus." Flavian was condemned unheard, and his fall must have involved the collapse of orthodoxy throughout the Eastern church—had that church been left to her own resources.

But outside that church was a religious and moral authority with which the "pharaohs" and the emperors had to reckon. Though in the struggle between the two Eastern patriarchates the Byzantine court always took the side of injustice and heresy, the cause of justice and orthodoxy, whether maintained by Alexandria or Constantinople, never failed to find vigorous support in the Apostolic See of Rome.

The contrast is indeed striking. It is the Emperor Constantius who ruthlessly persecutes Athanasius; it is Pope Julius who takes his part and defends him against the whole East. It is Pope Inno-

---

[7] A curious fact, and one which strikingly confirms our theory of the partiality of the Byzantine emperors for heresy *as such*, is that the same Emperor Theodosius II, who had favored the Nestorian heresy and had seen it condemned by the Church in spite of his efforts, became subsequently the enthusiastic supporter of Eutyches and Dioscorus who held the view diametrically opposite to that of Nestorius, though no less heretical.

cent who makes energetic protest against the persecution of John Chrysostom and, after the death of the saint, takes the first step toward the rehabilitation of his memory in the Church. Again, it is Pope Celestine who backs Cyril with all the weight of his authority in his courageous struggle against the heresy of Nestorius and its political champions; and there can be no doubt that, without the aid of the Apostolic See, the patriarch of Alexandria, for all his energy, would not have succeeded in overcoming the combined forces of the imperial power and the greater part of the Greek clergy.

This contrast between the policy of the empire and that of the papacy may be observed right through the history of the Eastern heresies, which were not only invariably supported but sometimes even invented by the emperors, as the Monothelite heresy was by the Emperor Heraclius and the Iconoclastic heresy by Leo the Isaurian. But we must pause at the fifth century over the struggle of the two patriarchates and the instructive history of the "robber-council" of Ephesus.

Repeated experience had proved that in the quarrel between the two princes of the Eastern church, the Western pope showed no bias or partiality, but invariably gave his support to the cause of justice and truth. Accordingly, the tyrant and heretic Dioscorus could not count on Rome for the same assistance that his predecessor Cyril had received. His plan was to secure primacy over the whole Eastern church by the condemnation of Flavian and the triumph of the Egyptian faction, more or less Monophysite, of which he himself was the leader. Realizing that there was no hope of the pope's consent being given to such a plan, he resolved to achieve his object without the pope or, if necessary, in spite of him.

In 449, a council which was ecumenical in its composition assembled at Ephesus. The whole Eastern church was represented. The legates of Pope Leo were also present, but were not allowed to preside over the council. Dioscorus, guarded by the imperial officers and attended by his Egyptian bishops and a mob of clerics armed with staffs, presided like a king holding court. The bishops of the orthodox party were cowed and silent. "All of them," we read in the Russian Martyrology (life of St. Flavian), "loved darkness rather than light and preferred falsehood to truth, desiring rather to please their earthly king than the King of heaven."

Flavian had to submit to a farcical trial. Some of the bishops threw themselves at Dioscorus' feet and implored his indulgence for the accused. The Egyptians handled them roughly amid deafening cries of "Hack asunder those who would divide Christ!" The orthodox bishops were given tablets on which nothing was written and to which they were compelled to put their signatures, knowing that a heretical formula would be immediately inscribed upon them. The majority signed without a murmur. A few desired to sign with certain reservations, but the Egyptian clergy tore the tablets from their hands, breaking their fingers with blows from their staffs. Finally, Dioscorus arose and in the name of the council pronounced sentence of condemnation against Flavian, who was deposed, excommunicated, and handed over to the secular arm. Flavian tried to protest, but Dioscorus' clerics fell on him and handled him so roughly that he died within two days.

When injustice, violence, and falsehood thus reigned supreme in an ecumenical council, where was the infallible and inviolable Church of Christ? It was present and moreover gave proof of its presence. At the moment when Flavian was being done to death by the brutalities of Dioscorus' minions, when the heretical bishops were loudly acclaiming the triumph of their leader, while the orthodox bishops stood by, trembling and silent, Hilary, the deacon of the Roman Church, cried: "*Contradicitur!*" ["It is contradicted!"][8]

At that moment it was certainly not the cowering, silent crowd of orthodox Easterns which represented the Church of God. All the immortal power of the Church was concentrated for Eastern Christendom in that simple legal word spoken by the Roman deacon: *contradicitur.*

We are accustomed to find fault with the distinctively juridical

---

[8] Mansi, 6:908.

and legalistic character of the Western Church; and no doubt the principles and formulae of Roman law do not bind in the kingdom of God. But the "robber-council" of Ephesus was an express vindication of Latin justice. The *contradicitur* of the Roman deacon was the symbol of principle against current reality, of right against brute force, of unshakable moral stability against victorious wickedness on the one hand and cowardice on the other; it was, in a word, the impregnable rock of the Church against the gates of Hades.

The murderers of the patriarch of Constantinople did not dare to touch the deacon of the Roman Church. And in the short space of two years, the *contradicitur* of Rome had changed "the most holy Ecumenical Council of Ephesus" into the "robber-council" of Ephesus, had ousted the mitred assassin, decreed the canonization of his victim, and brought about the assembling of the true Ecumenical Council of Chalcedon under the presidency of the Roman legates.

Chapter 14

The Council of Chalcedon

The central authority of the universal Church is the impregnable foundation of social justice because it is the infallible organ of religious truth.

Pope Leo had a twofold task to accomplish: he had not only to reestablish in the Christian East the moral order which had been subverted by the misdeeds of the patriarch of Alexandria, but also to confirm his Eastern brethren in the true faith which was threatened by the heresy of Monophysitism. The distinctive truth of Christianity, the truth of the God-Man, was at stake.

The Monophysites, in asserting that the humanity of Jesus Christ was entirely absorbed by his divinity and that therefore after the Incarnation he was God alone, were reverting, unconsciously no doubt, to the inhuman god of Eastern paganism, the god who devours all that he has created and is nothing but an abyss unfathomable to the human spirit. Their assertion was ultimately a disguised denial of any permanent revelation or Incarnation, but it took shelter behind the great theological reputation of Cyril, who had let an inaccurate phrase fall from his pen in vindicating the unity of the person of Jesus Christ against Nestorius: one incarnate nature of God the Word. And because the denial of the faith was so disguised, it was necessary to find a new formula to express the truth of the divine humanity in clear and precise terms.

The whole orthodox world was awaiting such a formula from the successor of Peter. Pope Leo himself was profoundly aware of the importance of the question. "Jesus Christ, the Savior of mankind," he says, in founding the faith which recalls the wicked to righteousness and the dead to life, instilled into the minds of his disciples the exhortations of his teaching and the marvels of his works that the one Christ might be acknowledged both as the only-begotten of God and as the Son of Man. For one belief without the other was of no avail to salvation, and it was equally perilous to believe the Lord Jesus Christ to be God alone and not man, or to be man alone and not God

—since the former belief places him out of reach of our infirmity and the latter makes him unable to effect our salvation—

but both were to be confessed, for just as true humanity existed in the Godhead, so true divinity existed in the manhood.

In order therefore to confirm them in their most wholesome knowledge of this faith, the Lord had questioned his disciples: and the apostle Peter, surpassing the things of the body and transcending human knowledge by the revelation of the Spirit of the Father, beheld with the eyes of his mind the Son of the living God and acknowledged the glory of the Godhead because he did not look merely at the substance of flesh and blood. And Christ so approved the sublime faith of Peter that he pronounced him blessed and endowed him with the sacred stability of the inviolable rock on which the Church should be built to prevail against the gates of Hades and the jaws of death; so that in the decision of all causes, nothing shall be ratified in heaven but that which has been established by the judgment of Peter.[1]

Claiming, as he does, that the primary function of the authority of the Church—that of asserting and defining Christian truth—belongs for all time to the Chair of Peter which he occupies, Leo considers it his duty to combat the new heresy by expounding anew the confession of the apostle. In penning his famous dogmatic epistle to Flavian, he regards himself as the inspired interpreter of the prince of the apostles; and the whole orthodox East regarded him in the same light.

---

[1] *Works* (ed. Migne), 1:309.

In the *Leimonarion*[2] of St. Sophronius, patriarch of Jerusalem in the seventh century, we find the following legend: When Leo had written his epistle to Flavian the bishop of Constantinople against the impious Eutyches and Nestorius, he placed it upon the tomb of the chief apostle Peter and with prayers, vigils, and fasts he entreated the sovereign apostle in these words: "If in the frailty of human nature I have been guilty of error, do thou, to whom Jesus Christ our Savior, Lord, and God has entrusted this throne and the whole Church, supply every defect in what I have written and remove all that is superfluous." After forty days had elapsed, the apostle appeared to Leo while he was praying and said: "I have read and corrected it." And, taking up his epistle from the tomb of blessed Peter, Leo opened it and found it corrected by the apostle's hand.[3]

This epistle, truly worthy of such a reviser, defined with wonderful clarity and vigor the truth of the two natures in the one person of Christ, and thereafter left no place in the Church for the two opposite errors of Nestorius and Eutyches. That Leo's epistle was not read at the "robber-council" of Ephesus was the main reason urged for quashing the decrees of the pseudo-council. Though Dioscorus had succeeded in coercing the entire gathering of Eastern bishops into condemning Flavian and putting their names to a heretical document, he encountered unexpected opposition when he ventured on open rebellion against the Pope. For the latter, on receiving news from his legates of what had passed at Ephesus, at once convened a council of Latin bishops in Rome, and with their unanimous approval condemned and deposed Dioscorus.

The "pharaoh" who had returned to Alexandria in triumph attempted to outwit the Pope; he was soon to realize that it was no mere empty self-aggrandizement with which he was confronted, but a living spiritual authority which claimed the allegiance of the Christian conscience throughout the world. The pride and

---

[2] A kind of chrestomathy composed of edifying stories.

[3] See the life of St. Leo the Pope in the Russian Martyrology.

effrontery of the usurping bishop were shattered upon the true rock of the Church: employing all his customary methods of violence, Dioscorus succeeded in compelling only ten Egyptian bishops to lend their names to the condemnation of Pope Leo.[4] Even in the East this futile insult was universally regarded as an act of insanity, and it proved the final undoing of the Egyptian "pharaoh."

The Emperor Theodosius II, the champion of the two opposite heresies and the patron of both Nestorius and Dioscorus, had just died, and with the accession of Pulcheria and her nominal consort Marcian, there began a short phase during which the imperial government, apparently from religious conviction, ranged itself decisively upon the side of truth. In the East, this alone was enough to restore courage to the orthodox bishops and to enlist on the side of the true faith—which the new emperor professed —all those who had only sided with heresy to please his predecessor.

But the orthodox emperor himself had little confidence in these pliant prelates. For him, supreme authority in matters of faith belonged to the pope. "In all that concerns the Catholic religion and the faith of Christians," we read in a letter of his to Leo, "we have thought it right to approach in the first place Your Holiness who is the overseer and guardian of the divine faith."[5] According to the emperor's view, it is by the pope's authority that the forthcoming council must banish all impiety and error from the Church and establish perfect peace among all the bishops of the Catholic faith.[6] And in another letter which follows close upon the first, the emperor asserts again that the duty of the council will be to acknowledge and expound for the East what the pope has decreed at Rome.[7] The Empress Pulcheria uses the same language in her assurance to the Pope that the council "will define

---

[4] Mansi, 6:510.
[5] Ibid., 93.
[6] Loc. cit.
[7] Ibid., 100.

the Catholic belief by your authority, as Christian faith and piety require."[8]

When the ecumenical council had assembled at Chalcedon in 451 under the presidency of the Roman legates, Bishop Paschasinus, who was the principal legate, arose and said: "We bear instructions from the blessed and apostolic bishop of the city of Rome, who is the head of all the churches, forbidding us to admit Dioscorus to the deliberations of the council."[9] And the second legate, Lucentius, explained that Dioscorus was already condemned for having usurped judicial powers and having assembled a council without the consent of the Apostolic See, a thing which had never happened before and was forbidden.[10]

After considerable discussion, the emperor's representatives announced that Dioscorus would not sit as a member of the council but would appear as an accused man, since he had incurred accusation on fresh counts subsequent to his condemnation by the Pope.[11] Judgment upon him was withheld until after the reading of the Pope's dogmatic epistle, which the orthodox bishops hailed with shouts of: "Peter has spoken by the mouth of Leo!"[12]

In the following session, several members of the clergy of the church of Alexandria presented a petition addressed "to the most holy Leo, beloved of God, universal archbishop and patriarch of great Rome, and to the holy ecumenical council at Chalcedon." It was a bill of accusation against Dioscorus who, after ratifying heresy in a council of brigands and murdering Flavian, the complainants alleged, "attempted a still greater wickedness": the excommunication of the most holy and sacred Apostolic See of great Rome.[13]

---

[8] Ibid., 101.
[9] Ibid., 580–581.
[10] Ibid., 645.
[11] Loc. cit.
[12] Ibid., 972.
[13] Ibid., 1005–1009.

The council did not think itself competent to pass a fresh decision on a bishop whom the Pope had already judged, and it was proposed that the Roman legates should pronounce judgment on Dioscorus.[14] They did so accordingly, having first enumerated all the crimes of the patriarch of Alexandria in these terms:

> The most holy and blessed archbishop of great and old Rome, Leo, through us and the holy council here present, and together with the thrice-blessed and most glorious apostle Peter who is the rock and base of the Catholic Church and the foundation of the orthodox faith, has deprived the said Dioscorus of episcopal status and expelled him entirely from his priestly office.[15]

The solemn recognition of the pope's supreme authority at the Council of Chalcedon was sealed by the letter of the Eastern bishops to Leo, in which they attributed to him the merit of all that had been done at the council. "It is you," they wrote, "who through your legates have guided and ruled the whole gathering of the fathers, as the head rules the members, by showing them the true meaning of the dogma."[16]

It is clear that to reject the supremacy and doctrinal authority of the Roman See as usurped and false involves not merely a charge of usurpation and heresy against a man of the character of Leo the Great; it means accusing the Ecumenical Council of Chalcedon of heresy, and with it the whole orthodox Church of the fifth century. This is the conclusion that emerges unmistakably from the authentic evidence which the reader has had set before him.

---

[14] Ibid., 1045.
[15] Ibid., 1048.
[16] Ibid., 148.

PART FOUR

The Pope, the Universal Father

As God in his Trinity of Persons possesses absolutely the fullness of his divine substance, his heavenly body or his essential wisdom, so too the God-Man in the trinity of his messianic powers possesses completely the universal Church, his divine-human body, at once heavenly and earthly, the perfect spouse of the incarnate Word. "All power in heaven and on earth has been given to me" (Matt. 28:18).

This universal power is not the omnipotence of God; that belongs eternally to the Word and so cannot be given to him. The power here referred to is the messianic power of the God-Man, a power that does not relate to the universe outside God as such, but to the universe reunited to God, cooperating with him and incarnating in time his eternal essence. If the fullness of this power belongs by right to Christ and only to him, since he alone could merit it, the exercise of this divine-human power demands the free submission and the living cooperation of mankind itself. The action of Christ is therefore determined here by the progressive development of humanity, drawn by degrees into the divine-human sphere, assimilated to the Mystical Body of Christ, and transformed into the universal Church.

If God, that is to say, Christ in glory, had wished to impose his truth and his will upon men in a direct and supranatural manner, if he had wished to save the world by force, he could well have done so; just as before his glorification he could have asked his heavenly Father to send him a legion of angels to protect him from the servants of Caiaphas and the soldiers of Pilate. In that case, the history of the world would have been soon completed, but it would not have achieved its goal; there would have been no free cooperation between man and God, no true union and perfect concurrence between the creature and the Creator, and mankind itself, in losing its freedom of choice, would have been assimilated to the physical world.

But the divine Word did not become incarnate on earth in order to sanction materialism. Since that Incarnation, the freedom of man remains assured; the universal Church has a history. It was necessary that Christ should ascend to the heavens and govern the

Church by means of human ministers to whom he might delegate the moral and juridical fullness of the three messianic powers, without thereby imparting to them the immediate efficacy of his omnipotence which would have restricted the freedom of men. In a word, we know that in founding the Church Christ delegated his powers to her; and in doing so, he followed what we may call the trinitary scheme, *ratio Trinitatis*.

The Trinity of God is the evolution of absolute unity, which contains in itself all the fullness of being, unfolding itself in three hypostatized modes of the divine existence. We know that in the Trinity absolute unity is secured: 1) by the ontological primacy of the first hypostasis which is the original cause or principle of the two others, but not vice versa; 2) by the consubstantiality of all three, ensuring the indivisibility of their being; and 3) by their perfect solidarity which does not permit of their acting separately.

The social trinity of the universal Church is the evolution of the ecclesiastical monarchy, which contains in itself all the fullness of the messianic powers, unfolding itself in the three forms of Christian sovereignty. As in the Godhead, the unity of the universal Church is secured: 1) by the absolute primacy of the first of these three powers, the pontificate, which is the only sovereignty directly and immediately instituted by God and therefore de jure the cause and necessary condition of the two others; 2) by the essential community of these three powers as included within the same Body of Christ and sharing the same substance of religion, the same faith, tradition, and sacraments; 3) by the moral solidarity or community of aim, which for all three can be nothing but the coming of the kingdom of God, the perfect manifestation of the universal Church.

The religious community and moral solidarity of the three sovereign powers under the absolute primacy of the universal pontificate—such is the supreme law, the ultimate ideal of social Christendom. But though in God the trinitary form of unity exists in actuality from all eternity, in the Church it is only gradually realized. Hence, there is not only a difference, but even a certain contrast between the divine Trinity and the social trinity.

The primary aspect of the divine existence is absolute unity, of which the Trinity is the direct, perfect, and therefore eternal unfolding. The primary aspect of the Church is, on the contrary, the indeterminate plurality of natural, fallen humanity. In the divine being, the Trinity is the form by which absolute unity extends and unfolds itself; in the social being of the human race, the trinity is the form by which the indeterminate plurality of particular elements is reduced to a synthetic unity. Thus, the development of the Church is a process of unification within an ideally constant but actually variable relationship between de jure unity and de facto plurality, a process which involves two main operations: the progressive centralization of the given ecclesiastical body, and the unifying and synthetic action of the centralized Church, which aims at the incorporation of the whole of mankind into itself.

The hypostases of the divine Trinity are absolutely simple in themselves, and their trinitary relationship is perfectly pure and immediate. The sovereign powers of the trinitary society of the universal Church are simple neither in themselves nor in the conditions in which they must be realized. They are not simple in themselves, for they are only relative centers of a collective whole. The mode of their realization is complicated not only because of the indeterminate plurality of the human medium in which they must manifest themselves, but because the perfect messianic revelation finds in natural humanity only partially successful attempts at unification, upon which the unifying work of the Church must be grafted. While this materially assists the divine-human operation, it also imparts to it a less pure, regular, and harmonious character. The chaos which is only veiled by physical creation still asserts its claims not only in the history of natural humanity, but in the history of religion and of the Church as well.

The aim of the divine-human work is to save all men equally, to transform the whole world into a royal and prophetic priesthood, a society of God in which men find themselves in direct relation to Christ and have no need of sun (that is, of a special priesthood), of moon (that is, of a special kingship), or of stars (that is, of prophecy as a public function). But to attain this end, it is not enough to define it. It is only too obvious that the mass of men do not individually and subjectively possess piety, justice, and wisdom in sufficient measure to enter into direct contact with the Godhead or to invest each individual with the character of priest, king, and prophet. Hence it is necessary that these three messianic attributes should be permanently differentiated in the universal organism in order that Christ may have specific organs of his activity as priest, king, and prophet.

The people of Israel said to Moses at the foot of Sinai:

> "We cannot endure the presence of Yahweh, we shall all die. Go thou in our stead to speak with Yahweh, and thou shalt bring back all that he shall say to thee for us: so shalt thou be a mediator between us and the Most High, that we may live." And the Lord said to Moses: "What this people have said, they have well said" (cf. Ex. 20:19).

And by the command of Yahweh, Moses not only acted personally as a mediator between the Godhead and the people, but also, in declaring that the people had been called to be a priestly kingdom, he founded the three powers through which Yahweh was to exercise his social activity in Israel.

The human mediator of the Old Testament thus foreshadowed the divine-human mediator of the New Covenant. Jesus Christ, while preaching the kingdom of heaven (which is within us), grace, and truth, and proclaiming the perfect unity of love and freedom as the supreme law of his Church, nonetheless proceeds to organize the ecclesiastical body and to bestow upon it a central organ by the method of a special choice. All must be completely equal, all must be one, and yet there are only twelve apostles to whom the power of Christ is delegated, and among them there is only one on whom this power is conferred completely and absolutely.

We know that the principle of chaotic existence, of existence, that is to say, apart from the Godhead, is manifested in the life of natural humanity by the indeterminate succession of generations, in which the present hastens to supplant the past, only to be itself continually supplanted by an illusory and transient future. The parricidal children, becoming fathers, cannot but beget a new generation of parricides, and so on to infinity. Such is the evil law of mortal life. Therefore, if mankind is to be regenerated and given true life, its past must above all be stabilized by the organization of a permanent fatherhood.

Purely human society already allots to the transitory fatherhood of natural life three distinct functions: the father produces and sustains the *existence* of the child by begetting him and providing for his material needs; the father guides the moral and intellectual *development* of the adolescent by educating him; finally, the father remains for his grown son the living and venerable *memory* of his past. The first relationship is, for the child, one of complete *dependence*; the second lays upon the adolescent the duty of *obedience*; the third only demands filial *piety*, a free sentiment of veneration and a mutual friendship.

If, in family life, fatherhood is seen under these three successive aspects, in the regenerate social life of the whole human race it assumes them simultaneously. For there are always individuals and nations that have yet to be begotten to spiritual life and have yet to receive the elements of religious nurture—nations and individuals in moral and intellectual infancy. Others, like adolescents, must in every age develop their spiritual powers and faculties with a certain freedom, but nonetheless must be constantly watched over and guided on the true path by the authority of a father, which shows itself at this stage mainly as an educative and teaching authority. Finally, there are always, if not whole nations, at least individuals who have reached spiritual maturity, and the more conscious and freer they are, the greater is the veneration and filial piety they feel for spiritual fatherhood.

From another point of view, there is bound to be a hierarchical gradation in spiritual fatherhood in proportion to the extent of the social units which it embraces. We know that the Church is natural humanity transubstantiated. Now, natural humanity is constituted on the analogy of a living body. A physical body is a complex unity made up of relatively simple elements of different degrees in a complicated relationship of subordination and coordination. The main degrees of this physical hierarchy are three in number. The lowest degree is represented by the relatively simple units, the elementary organs or organic elements of the body. In the middle degree we find the limbs of the body and its organs properly so-called, which are more or less composite. Finally, all these members and organs are subordinate to the unity of the whole body controlled by a central organ.

Similarly, in the political organism of natural humanity, which Christianity was to regenerate, relatively simple units—tribes, clans, rural communities, small states—were united in composite collectives more or less subdivided: nations at different stages of development, provinces of varying extent. Finally, all the provinces and nations were united in the universal monarchy, governed by a unique social organ, the city of Rome, a city which concentrated in itself the whole world and was at once *urbs et orbis* [city and world].

This was the organism which Christianity was to transubstantiate. The body of historic humanity was to be regenerated in every part in accordance with the order of its composition. And since Christ established a spiritual fatherhood as the basis of this regeneration, that fatherhood had to take form in accordance with the given variations in the forms of society.

There were, therefore, three degrees in the spiritual fatherhood or the priesthood: each primary social community or village, transubstantiated into a parish, received a spiritual father or priest; and all these priests together formed the lower clergy or the priesthood properly speaking. The provinces of the empire, transubstantiated into eparchies or dioceses of different orders, each formed a large family with a common father in the person of the *archiereus* or bishop, the immediate father of the priests under him and, through them, of all the faithful of his diocese. But all the spiritual social units of this second order represented by the episcopate, the particular churches of cities, provinces, and nations governed by prelates of all degrees (simple bishops, archbishops, metropolitans, primates, or patriarchs), are only members of the universal

Church which must itself be manifest as a higher unit embracing all these members.

The mere juxtaposition of its parts is not in fact enough to constitute a living body. It must possess a formal unity or substantial form which definitely embraces in actuality all the particular units, the elements and organs of which the body is composed. And if the particular spiritual families—which, among them, make up mankind—are in reality to form a single Christian family, a single universal Church, they must be subject to a common fatherhood embracing all Christian nations. To assert that there exist in reality nothing more than national churches is to assert that the members of a body exist in and for themselves and that the body itself does not have reality. On the contrary, Christ did not found any particular church. He created them all in the real unity of the universal Church which he entrusted to Peter as the one supreme representative of the divine fatherhood to the whole family of the sons of man.

It was by no mere chance that Jesus Christ specially ascribed to the first divine hypostasis, the heavenly Father, that divine-human act which made Simon Bar-Jona the first social father of the whole human family and the infallible master of the school of mankind. "Flesh and blood has not revealed this to you, but my Father who is in heaven" (Matt. 16:17). God the Holy Trinity is as indivisible in his action toward outside things as in his inner life. If Peter was divinely inspired, it was by God the Son and God the Holy Spirit as much as by God the Father, and since it was a matter of inspiration, it might have seemed more appropriate to make special mention of the Holy Spirit who spoke through the prophets.

But it is just here that we see the divine reason which governed every word of Christ, and the universal significance of his utterance to Peter. For it was not a matter of asserting that in this particular instance Simon had been inspired from above; that was as possible for him as for any of his fellows. Rather, it was a matter of establishing in his favor the unique institution of universal fatherhood in the Church, the image and instrument of the divine fatherhood. Therefore, it was above all to the heavenly Father that

the supreme reason and sanction for this institution was to be referred.

It is hard to leave the pure air of the Galilean mountains for
the polluted atmosphere of the Dead Sea. Our anti-Catholic controversialists, while admitting that the church of the parish or of
the diocese needs its priest or bishop, its visible father, the human organ of the divine fatherhood, will hear nothing of a common father for the whole universal Church. The only head of the
Church, they say, is Jesus Christ. And yet they see no reason why
a parish or a diocese should not be governed by a visible minister;
every Orthodox is ready to see in each bishop or priest a vicar of
Jesus Christ, though he cries "Blasphemy!" when Catholics give
this title to the first of the patriarchs, the successor of Peter.

But do these Orthodox schismatics in fact recognize Jesus
Christ as head of the Church? If he were really for them the
sovereign head, they would obey his words. Is it obedience to
the Master that drives them into rebellion against the steward that
he has himself appointed? They are ready to allow Christ to act
through his ministers in any given part of his visible kingdom,
but they appear to think that he exceeded the limits of his power
and abused his rights in giving to Peter the keys of the whole
kingdom. It is as though an English subject, while allowing the
empress of India the right of nominating a governor at Madras
and a magistrate at Bombay, were to dispute her appointment of
the viceroy at Calcutta.

But, it may be said, the universal Church in her entirety goes
beyond the bounds of earthly humanity; she includes the saints
in paradise, the souls in purgatory, and even, adds Khomyakov,
the souls of those yet unborn. We doubt whether the pope is
much concerned to extend his jurisdiction over the souls of the
unborn. But, speaking seriously, we are not dealing with the universal Church in its absolute and eternal totality, but in its relative and temporal totality, with the visible Church in each given
moment of its historic existence. For the Church, as for the individual man, there is the invisible totality, or the soul, and the
visible totality, or the body. The soul of man surpasses the limits

of earthly existence, it survives the physical organism, and in the world of spirits it thinks and acts without the medium of a material brain; but if anyone were to draw from that the conclusion that in his earthly existence man can get along without brains, the conclusion would hardly be granted, except perhaps in his own case!

There is another *a priori* argument used to evade the necessity for a universal fatherhood. Since the principle of fatherhood represents tradition, the memory of the past, it is thought to be enough for the Church to show true spiritual fatherhood by guarding tradition and preserving the memory of its own past. From this point of view, spiritual fatherhood would be represented solely by the great departed ancestors of religious society, the Fathers of the Church.

But why not extend this logic to particular churches? Why are not the faithful of a parish content to find this spiritual fatherhood in the historic memory of the first founders of their parish church? Why do they also need a living spiritual father, a permanent parish priest? And why does it not completely satisfy the inhabitants of Moscow to have a sacred tradition, a pious remembrance of the first rulers of their church, the holy metropolitans Peter and Alexis? Why do they also want a living bishop as a perpetual representative of this ancient tradition?

To relegate the spiritual fatherhood of the Church to the past (in the proper sense of that which has only an ideal existence for us) is to misconceive her very essence and raison d'être. The barbarous ancestors of mankind knew better: they recognized the survival of ancestors and even made them the main object of their worship, but for the continual maintenance of that worship they required that the dead ancestor should always have a living successor, the soul of the family, the priest or sacrificer, the permanent intermediary between the invisible divinity and their actual life.

Without a single father common to the whole human family, the earthly life of the sons of Adam must remain subject to division of every kind, and unity will have only an ideal existence upon earth. Real unity will be driven back to heaven like the legendary Astraea,[1] and chaos will reign upon the earth. In that case, Christianity would have failed; for it is in order to unify the lower world, to draw the earth out of chaos and unite it with the heavens, that the Word was made flesh. The docetic Christ of the Gnostics, a phantom Christ, would be more than sufficient to found an invisible church. But the real Christ has founded a real Church upon earth and has based it upon a permanent fatherhood universally diffused throughout all the parts of the social organism, but actually concentrated, for the whole body, in the person of the common father of all the faithful, the supreme pontiff, the elder or presbyter par excellence, the pope.

The pope as such is directly the father of all the bishops and, through them, of all the priests. Thus he is father of fathers. There is no question that the pope is the only bishop to be called not only "brother" but "father" by other bishops from the earliest times; and it was not only individual bishops that recognized his paternal authority, but gatherings of the whole episcopate as impressive, for instance, as the Council of Chalcedon.

But this fatherhood of the pope in relation to the teaching Church or the clergy does not belong to him absolutely. Not only bishops, but all priests are, under certain aspects, the equals of the pope. The pope has no essential preeminence over a simple priest in the ministry of the sacraments, with the exception of holy orders, in which he has no privilege above that of any other bishop. For this reason, the pope calls the bishops not only his sons but also his brothers, and is called brother by them.

Thus, within the limits of the Church properly speaking, the pope has only a relative fatherhood, not fully analogous to the divine fatherhood. The essential characteristic of the latter is that the Father is such in an absolutely unique manner, that he alone is Father, and that the Son and the Spirit, while partaking in the Godhead, do not partake in the divine fatherhood in any manner or degree. But the bishops and priests—the whole teaching Church—share more or less in the spiritual fatherhood of the

---

[1] The goddess of justice in Greek mythology.—ED.

pope. Fundamentally, there is no essential difference between this spiritual fatherhood or priestly power in the pope and the same power as it is in the bishops; just as the power of the episcopate is the relative fullness of the power of the priesthood, so its absolute fullness is found in the papacy.